THE

FAMILY TREE

OUR FAMILY TREE INDEX

Greetings Family Historian,

In your hands, you hold the world's first-ever 12 generation family history notebook. It contains everything you need to create an index of the first 4,095 people in your family! A numbered chart system makes it easy to see how the pages connect, and there are extra areas to write about historic events that your family members may have experienced. Use the prompts on each page to fill in the blanks as you solve mysteries and discover lost ancestors. This journal is here to help you create a personalized family heirloom that can be treasured for generations!

Yours Truly,
House Elves Anonymous

CONTENTS

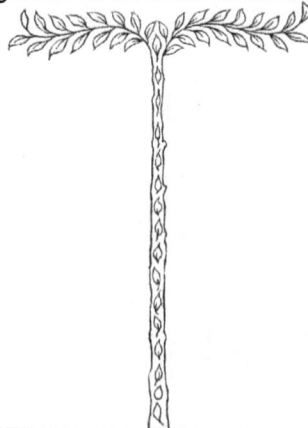

HOUSE ELVES ANONYMOUS

This book is dedicated to my musical Mom Jeany, and to my dear uncles, Ray Kurdziel, Howard Zar, and Harvey Zar, who first sparked my interest in genealogy. Thank you for sharing your love of culture and historic objects with my brother and me. I hope this book will help continue that tradition in other families, all around the world. With love, S. Zar

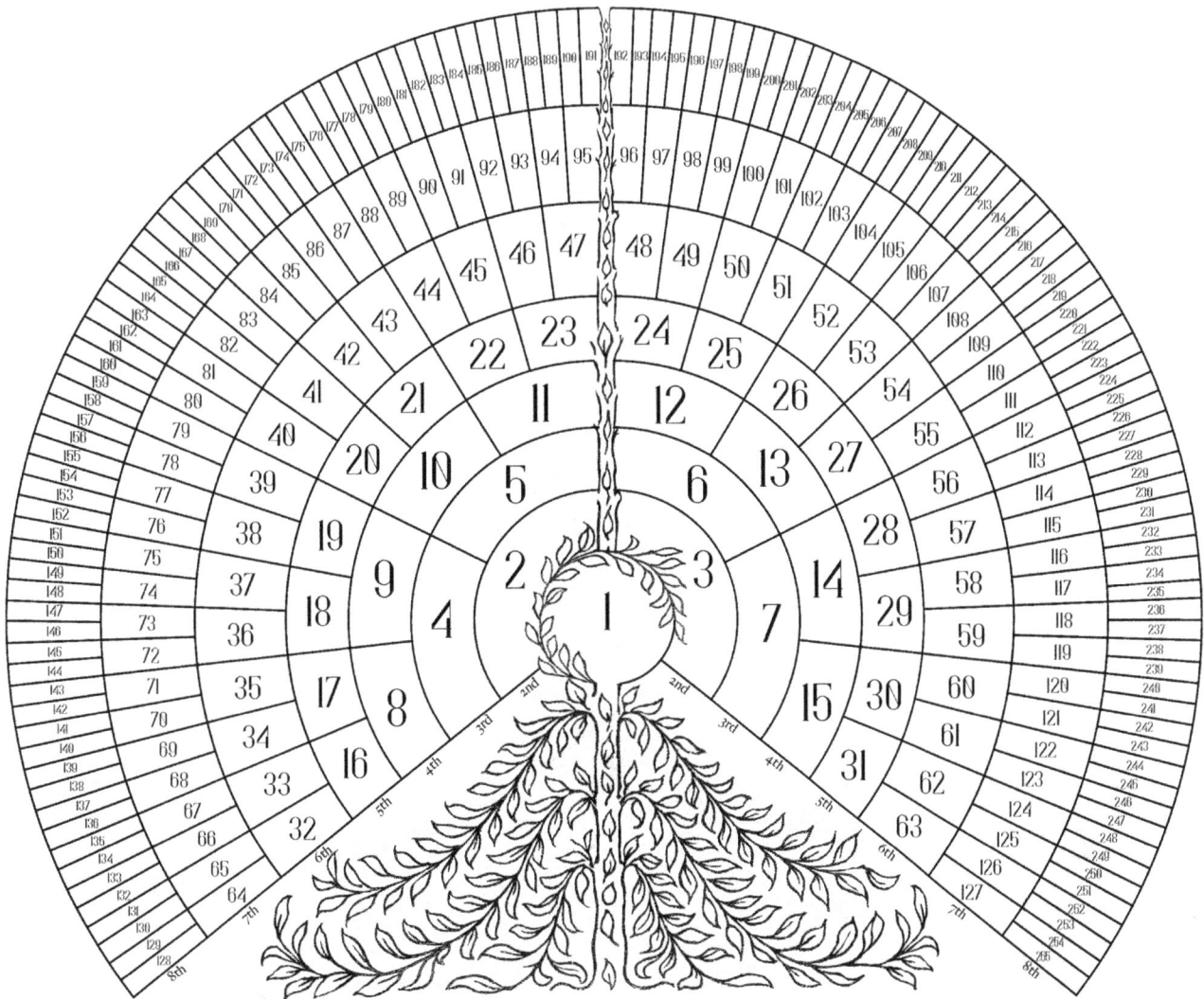

INTRODUCTION

HOW TO USE THIS FAMILY TREE BOOK

Each number in the tree above corresponds to a numbered area in this book for each of your ancestors. (There are larger versions of this chart on the next page and at HouseElvesAnonymous.com, where you can download it for free.) On the page marked **1**, you can write in the youngest person (or group of siblings) in your family tree. After that, you can refer to the chart as you add in more ancestors. The even numbers are for men, and the odd numbers are for women.

Recording your family history is a deeply personal and meaningful adventure, and this book strives to give you as much free-writing space as possible for each person. You can write in things like interesting historical notes, occupations, favorite quotes, hobbies, or how the couple fell in love!

Some people like to use this book to get organized before filling in their family tree by hand. The matching family tree chart is also available on our website.

1

2nd

3rd

4th

5th

6th

7th

8th

3

6

7

12

13

14

15

24

25

26

27

28

29

30

31

48

49

50

51

52

53

54

55

56

57

58

59

60

61

62

63

96

97

98

99

100

101

102

103

104

105

106

107

108

109

110

111

112

113

114

115

116

117

118

119

120

121

122

123

124

125

126

127

192

193

194

195

196

197

198

199

200

201

202

203

204

205

206

207

208

209

210

211

212

213

214

215

216

217

218

219

220

221

222

223

224

225

226

227

228

229

230

231

232

233

234

235

236

237

238

239

240

241

242

243

244

245

246

247

248

249

250

251

252

253

254

255

THE
ANCESTRY OF

In the wreath at the top, you can write in the youngest person or group of siblings in the family. Use the area above (and on the next page) to write in important details, such as birthdays, talents, locations, etc. This first generation represents position ONE in the chart. The parents will be recorded in positions 2 and 3, and so on.

THE
ANCESTRY OF

CONTINUED...

2

PARENT

NAME

BORN

DIED

MARRIED

NOTES

3

PARENT

NAME

BORN

DIED

MARRIED

NOTES

THE
3rd
GENERATION
GRANDPARENTS

HISTORIC EVENTS THIS GENERATION EXPERIENCED:

THE
3rd
GENERATION
GRANDPARENTS

4
GRANDFATHER

NAME

BORN

DIED

MARRIED

NOTES

5

GRANDMOTHER

NAME

BORN

DIED

MARRIED

NOTES

6

GRANDFATHER

NAME

BORN

DIED

MARRIED

NOTES

7

GRANDMOTHER

NAME

BORN

DIED

MARRIED

NOTES

THE
4th
GENERATION
GREAT-GRANDPARENTS

HISTORIC EVENTS THIS GENERATION EXPERIENCED:

THE
4th
GENERATION
GREAT-GRANDPARENTS

8
GREAT-GRANDFATHER

NAME

BORN

DIED

MARRIED

NOTES

9
GREAT-GRANDMOTHER

NAME

BORN

DIED

MARRIED

NOTES

10
GREAT-GRANDFATHER

NAME

BORN

DIED

MARRIED

NOTES

11
GREAT-GRANDMOTHER

NAME

BORN

DIED

MARRIED

NOTES

12

GREAT-GRANDFATHER

NAME

BORN

DIED

MARRIED

NOTES

13

GREAT-GRANDMOTHER

NAME

BORN

DIED

MARRIED

NOTES

14

GREAT-GRANDFATHER

NAME

BORN

DIED

MARRIED

NOTES

15

GREAT-GRANDMOTHER

NAME

BORN

DIED

MARRIED

NOTES

THE
5th
GENERATION

GREAT-GREAT-GRANDPARENTS

HISTORIC EVENTS THIS GENERATION EXPERIENCED:

THE
5th
GENERATION
GREAT-GREAT-GRANDPARENTS

16

2X GREAT-GRANDFATHER

NAME

BORN

DIED

MARRIED

NOTES

17

2X GREAT-GRANDMOTHER

NAME

BORN

DIED

MARRIED

NOTES

18

2X GREAT-GRANDFATHER

NAME

BORN

DIED

MARRIED

NOTES

19

2X GREAT-GRANDMOTHER

NAME

BORN

DIED

MARRIED

NOTES

20

2X GREAT-GRANDFATHER

NAME

BORN

DIED

MARRIED

NOTES

21

2X GREAT-GRANDMOTHER

NAME

BORN

DIED

MARRIED

NOTES

22

2X GREAT-GRANDFATHER

NAME

BORN

DIED

MARRIED

NOTES

23

2X GREAT-GRANDMOTHER

NAME

BORN

DIED

MARRIED

NOTES

24

2X GREAT-GRANDFATHER

NAME

BORN

DIED

MARRIED

NOTES

25

2X GREAT-GRANDMOTHER

NAME

BORN

DIED

MARRIED

NOTES

26

2X GREAT-GRANDFATHER

NAME

BORN

DIED

MARRIED

NOTES

27

2X GREAT-GRANDMOTHER

NAME

BORN

DIED

MARRIED

NOTES

28

2X GREAT-GRANDFATHER

NAME

BORN

DIED

MARRIED

NOTES

29

2X GREAT-GRANDMOTHER

NAME

BORN

DIED

MARRIED

NOTES

30

2X GREAT-GRANDFATHER

NAME

BORN

DIED

MARRIED

NOTES

31

2X GREAT-GRANDMOTHER

NAME

BORN

DIED

MARRIED

NOTES

THE
6th
GENERATION
3X GREAT-GRANDPARENTS

HISTORIC EVENTS THIS GENERATION EXPERIENCED:

THE
6th
GENERATION

3X GREAT-GRANDPARENTS

32 & 33
3X GREAT-GRANDPARENTS

3X GREAT-GRANDFATHER

NAME

BORN

DIED

MARRIED

NOTES

3X GREAT-GRANDMOTHER

NAME

BORN

DIED

NOTES

34 & 35

3X GREAT-GRANDPARENTS

3X GREAT-GRANDFATHER

NAME

BORN

DIED

MARRIED

NOTES

3X GREAT-GRANDMOTHER

NAME

BORN

DIED

NOTES

36 & 37
3X GREAT-GRANDPARENTS

3X GREAT-GRANDFATHER

NAME

BORN

DIED

MARRIED

NOTES

3X GREAT-GRANDMOTHER

NAME

BORN

DIED

NOTES

38 & 39
3X GREAT-GRANDPARENTS

3X GREAT-GRANDFATHER

NAME

BORN

DIED

MARRIED

NOTES

3X GREAT-GRANDMOTHER

NAME

BORN

DIED

NOTES

40 & 41
3X GREAT-GRANDPARENTS

3X GREAT-GRANDFATHER

NAME

BORN

DIED

MARRIED

NOTES

3X GREAT-GRANDMOTHER

NAME

BORN

DIED

NOTES

42 & 43
3X GREAT-GRANDPARENTS

3X GREAT-GRANDFATHER

NAME

BORN

DIED

MARRIED

NOTES

3X GREAT-GRANDMOTHER

NAME

BORN

DIED

NOTES

44 & 45
3X GREAT-GRANDPARENTS

3X GREAT-GRANDFATHER

NAME

BORN

DIED

MARRIED

NOTES

3X GREAT-GRANDMOTHER

NAME

BORN

DIED

NOTES

46 & 47
3X GREAT-GRANDPARENTS

3X GREAT-GRANDFATHER

NAME

BORN

DIED

MARRIED

NOTES

3X GREAT-GRANDMOTHER

NAME

BORN

DIED

NOTES

48 & 49
3X GREAT-GRANDPARENTS

3X GREAT-GRANDFATHER

NAME

BORN

DIED

MARRIED

NOTES

3X GREAT-GRANDMOTHER

NAME

BORN

DIED

NOTES

50 & 51
3X GREAT-GRANDPARENTS

3X GREAT-GRANDFATHER

NAME

BORN

DIED

MARRIED

NOTES

3X GREAT-GRANDMOTHER

NAME

BORN

DIED

NOTES

52 & 53
3X GREAT-GRANDPARENTS

3X GREAT-GRANDFATHER

NAME

BORN

DIED

MARRIED

NOTES

3X GREAT-GRANDMOTHER

NAME

BORN

DIED

NOTES

54 & 55
3X GREAT-GRANDPARENTS

3X GREAT-GRANDFATHER

NAME

BORN

DIED

MARRIED

NOTES

3X GREAT-GRANDMOTHER

NAME

BORN

DIED

NOTES

56 & 57

3X GREAT-GRANDPARENTS

3X GREAT-GRANDFATHER

NAME

BORN

DIED

MARRIED

NOTES

3X GREAT-GRANDMOTHER

NAME

BORN

DIED

NOTES

58 & 59
3X GREAT-GRANDPARENTS

NAME

BORN

DIED

MARRIED

NOTES

NAME

BORN

DIED

NOTES

60 & 61

3X GREAT-GRANDPARENTS

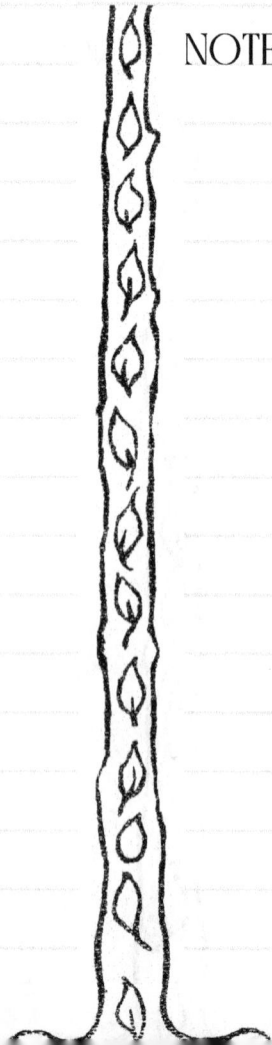

3X GREAT-GRANDFATHER

NAME

BORN

DIED

MARRIED

NOTES

3X GREAT-GRANDMOTHER

NAME

BORN

DIED

NOTES

62 & 63
3X GREAT-GRANDPARENTS

3X GREAT-GRANDFATHER

NAME

BORN

DIED

MARRIED

NOTES

3X GREAT-GRANDMOTHER

NAME

BORN

DIED

NOTES

THE
7th
GENERATION

4X GREAT-GRANDPARENTS

HISTORIC EVENTS THIS GENERATION EXPERIENCED:

THE
7th
GENERATION

4X GREAT-GRANDPARENTS

64 - 67
4X GREAT-GRANDPARENTS

64. 4X GREAT-GRANDFATHER

NAME

BORN

DIED

MARRIED

NOTES

65. 4X GREAT-GRANDMOTHER

NAME

BORN

DIED

NOTES

66. 4X GREAT-GRANDFATHER

NAME

BORN

DIED

MARRIED

NOTES

67. 4X GREAT-GRANDMOTHER

NAME

BORN

DIED

NOTES

68 - 71
4X GREAT-GRANDPARENTS

68. 4X GREAT-GRANDFATHER

NAME

BORN

DIED

MARRIED

NOTES

69. 4X GREAT-GRANDMOTHER

NAME

BORN

DIED

NOTES

70. 4X GREAT-GRANDFATHER

NAME

BORN

DIED

MARRIED

NOTES

71. 4X GREAT-GRANDMOTHER

NAME

BORN

DIED

NOTES

72 - 75
4X GREAT-GRANDPARENTS

72. 4X GREAT-GRANDFATHER

NAME

BORN

DIED

MARRIED

NOTES

73. 4X GREAT-GRANDMOTHER

NAME

BORN

DIED

NOTES

74. 4X GREAT-GRANDFATHER

NAME

BORN

DIED

MARRIED

NOTES

75. 4X GREAT-GRANDMOTHER

NAME

BORN

DIED

NOTES

76 - 79
4X GREAT-GRANDPARENTS

76. 4X GREAT-GRANDFATHER

NAME

BORN

DIED

MARRIED

NOTES

77. 4X GREAT-GRANDMOTHER

NAME

BORN

DIED

NOTES

78. 4X GREAT-GRANDFATHER

NAME

BORN

DIED

MARRIED

NOTES

79. 4X GREAT-GRANDMOTHER

NAME

BORN

DIED

NOTES

80 - 83
4X GREAT-GRANDPARENTS

80. 4X GREAT-GRANDFATHER

NAME

BORN

DIED

MARRIED

NOTES

81. 4X GREAT-GRANDMOTHER

NAME

BORN

DIED

NOTES

82. 4X GREAT-GRANDFATHER

NAME

BORN

DIED

MARRIED

NOTES

83. 4X GREAT-GRANDMOTHER

NAME

BORN

DIED

NOTES

84 - 87
4X GREAT-GRANDPARENTS

84. 4X GREAT-GRANDFATHER

NAME

BORN

DIED

MARRIED

NOTES

85. 4X GREAT-GRANDMOTHER

NAME

BORN

DIED

NOTES

86. 4X GREAT-GRANDFATHER

NAME

BORN

DIED

MARRIED

NOTES

87. 4X GREAT-GRANDMOTHER

NAME

BORN

DIED

NOTES

88 – 91
4X GREAT-GRANDPARENTS

88. 4X GREAT-GRANDFATHER

NAME

BORN

DIED

MARRIED

NOTES

89. 4X GREAT-GRANDMOTHER

NAME

BORN

DIED

NOTES

90. 4X GREAT-GRANDFATHER

NAME

BORN

DIED

MARRIED

NOTES

91. 4X GREAT-GRANDMOTHER

NAME

BORN

DIED

NOTES

92 – 95
4X GREAT-GRANDPARENTS

92. 4X GREAT-GRANDFATHER

NAME

BORN

DIED

MARRIED

NOTES

93. 4X GREAT-GRANDMOTHER

NAME

BORN

DIED

NOTES

94. 4X GREAT-GRANDFATHER

NAME

BORN

DIED

MARRIED

NOTES

95. 4X GREAT-GRANDMOTHER

NAME

BORN

DIED

NOTES

96 - 99
4X GREAT-GRANDPARENTS

96. 4X GREAT-GRANDFATHER

NAME

BORN

DIED

MARRIED

NOTES

97. 4X GREAT-GRANDMOTHER

NAME

BORN

DIED

NOTES

98. 4X GREAT-GRANDFATHER

NAME

BORN

DIED

MARRIED

NOTES

99. 4X GREAT-GRANDMOTHER

NAME

BORN

DIED

NOTES

100 – 103

4X GREAT-GRANDPARENTS

100. 4X GREAT-GRANDFATHER

NAME

BORN

DIED

MARRIED

NOTES

101. 4X GREAT-GRANDMOTHER

NAME

BORN

DIED

NOTES

102. 4X GREAT-GRANDFATHER

NAME

BORN

DIED

MARRIED

NOTES

103. 4X GREAT-GRANDMOTHER

NAME

BORN

DIED

NOTES

104 - 107
4X GREAT-GRANDPARENTS

104. 4X GREAT-GRANDFATHER

NAME

BORN

DIED

MARRIED

NOTES

105. 4X GREAT-GRANDMOTHER

NAME

BORN

DIED

NOTES

106. 4X GREAT-GRANDFATHER

NAME

BORN

DIED

MARRIED

NOTES

107. 4X GREAT-GRANDMOTHER

NAME

BORN

DIED

NOTES

108 - 111
4X GREAT-GRANDPARENTS

108. 4X GREAT-GRANDFATHER

NAME

BORN

DIED

MARRIED

NOTES

109. 4X GREAT-GRANDMOTHER

NAME

BORN

DIED

NOTES

110. 4X GREAT-GRANDFATHER

NAME

BORN

DIED

MARRIED

NOTES

111. 4X GREAT-GRANDMOTHER

NAME

BORN

DIED

NOTES

112 - 115
4X GREAT-GRANDPARENTS

112. 4X GREAT-GRANDFATHER

NAME

BORN

DIED

MARRIED

NOTES

113. 4X GREAT-GRANDMOTHER

NAME

BORN

DIED

NOTES

114. 4X GREAT-GRANDFATHER

NAME

BORN

DIED

MARRIED

NOTES

115. 4X GREAT-GRANDMOTHER

NAME

BORN

DIED

NOTES

116 – 119
4X GREAT-GRANDPARENTS

116. 4X GREAT-GRANDFATHER

NAME

BORN

DIED

MARRIED

NOTES

117. 4X GREAT-GRANDMOTHER

NAME

BORN

DIED

NOTES

118. 4X GREAT-GRANDFATHER

NAME

BORN

DIED

MARRIED

NOTES

119. 4X GREAT-GRANDMOTHER

NAME

BORN

DIED

NOTES

120 - 123

4X GREAT-GRANDPARENTS

120. 4X GREAT-GRANDFATHER

NAME

BORN

DIED

MARRIED

NOTES

121. 4X GREAT-GRANDMOTHER

NAME

BORN

DIED

NOTES

122. 4X GREAT-GRANDFATHER

NAME

BORN

DIED

MARRIED

NOTES

123. 4X GREAT-GRANDMOTHER

NAME

BORN

DIED

NOTES

124 - 127
4X GREAT-GRANDPARENTS

124. 4X GREAT-GRANDFATHER

NAME

BORN

DIED

MARRIED

NOTES

125. 4X GREAT-GRANDMOTHER

NAME

BORN

DIED

NOTES

126. 4X GREAT-GRANDFATHER

NAME

BORN

DIED

MARRIED

NOTES

127. 4X GREAT-GRANDMOTHER

NAME

BORN

DIED

NOTES

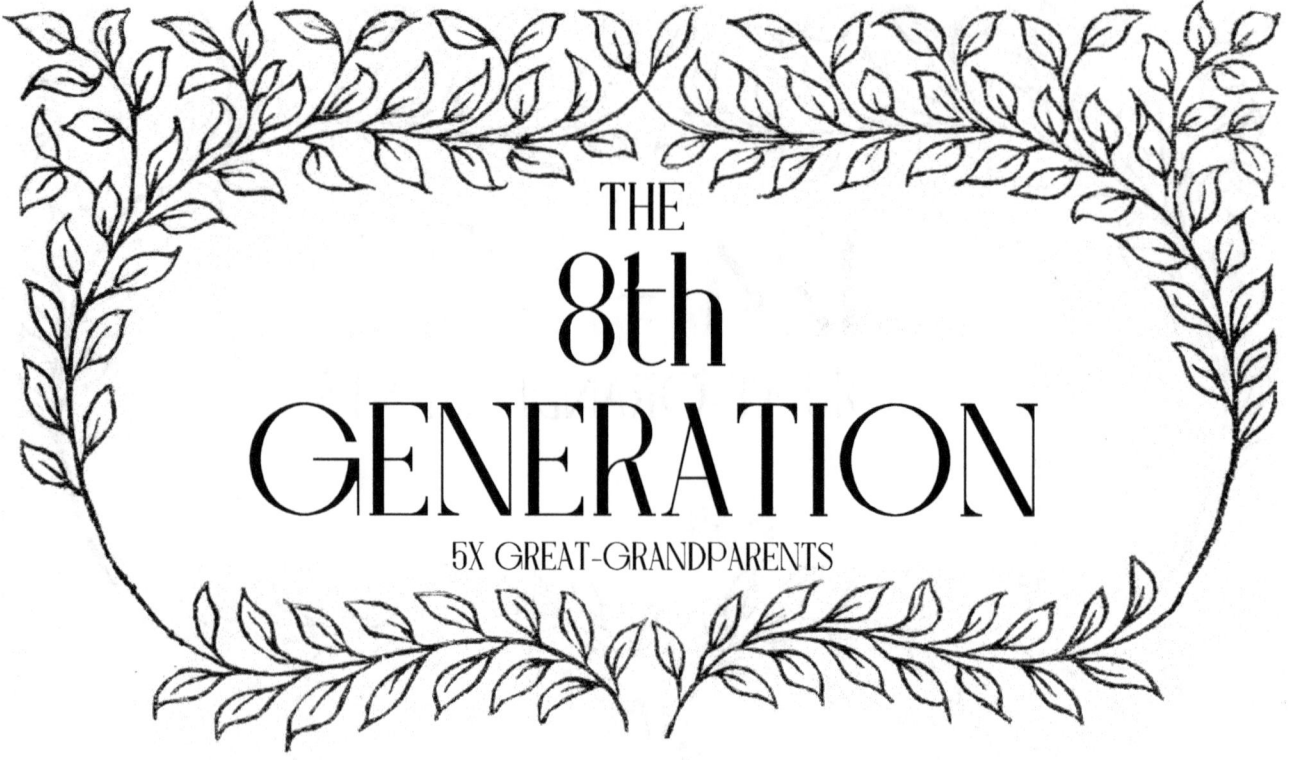

THE
8th
GENERATION

5X GREAT-GRANDPARENTS

HISTORIC EVENTS THIS GENERATION EXPERIENCED:

THE
8th
GENERATION

5X GREAT-GRANDPARENTS

128 – 135
5X GREAT-GRANDPARENTS

128. 5X GREAT-GRANDFATHER

NAME

BORN

DIED

MARRIED

129. 5X GREAT-GRANDMOTHER

NAME

BORN

DIED

130. 5X GREAT-GRANDFATHER

NAME

BORN

DIED

MARRIED

NOTES

131. 5X GREAT-GRANDMOTHER

NAME

BORN

DIED

NOTES

132. 5X GREAT-GRANDFATHER

NAME

BORN

DIED

MARRIED

133. 5X GREAT-GRANDMOTHER

NAME

BORN

DIED

134. 5X GREAT-GRANDFATHER

NAME

BORN

DIED

MARRIED

NOTES

135. 5X GREAT-GRANDMOTHER

NAME

BORN

DIED

NOTES

136 – 143
5X GREAT-GRANDPARENTS

136. 5X GREAT-GRANDFATHER
NAME

BORN

DIED

MARRIED

137. 5X GREAT-GRANDMOTHER
NAME

BORN

DIED

138. 5X GREAT-GRANDFATHER
NAME

BORN

DIED

MARRIED

NOTES

139. 5X GREAT-GRANDMOTHER
NAME

BORN

DIED

NOTES

140. 5X GREAT-GRANDFATHER
NAME

BORN

DIED

MARRIED

141. 5X GREAT-GRANDMOTHER
NAME

BORN

DIED

142. 5X GREAT-GRANDFATHER
NAME

BORN

DIED

MARRIED

NOTES

143. 5X GREAT-GRANDMOTHER
NAME

BORN

DIED

NOTES

144 – 151
5X GREAT-GRANDPARENTS

144. 5X GREAT-GRANDFATHER
NAME

BORN

DIED

MARRIED

145. 5X GREAT-GRANDMOTHER
NAME

BORN

DIED

146. 5X GREAT-GRANDFATHER
NAME

BORN

DIED

MARRIED

NOTES

147. 5X GREAT-GRANDMOTHER
NAME

BORN

DIED

NOTES

148. 5X GREAT-GRANDFATHER
NAME

BORN

DIED

MARRIED

149. 5X GREAT-GRANDMOTHER
NAME

BORN

DIED

150. 5X GREAT-GRANDFATHER
NAME

BORN

DIED

MARRIED

NOTES

151. 5X GREAT-GRANDMOTHER
NAME

BORN

DIED

NOTES

152 – 159
5X GREAT-GRANDPARENTS

152. 5X GREAT-GRANDFATHER

NAME

BORN

DIED

MARRIED

153. 5X GREAT-GRANDMOTHER

NAME

BORN

DIED

154. 5X GREAT-GRANDFATHER

NAME

BORN

DIED

MARRIED

NOTES

155. 5X GREAT-GRANDMOTHER

NAME

BORN

DIED

NOTES

156. 5X GREAT-GRANDFATHER

NAME

BORN

DIED

MARRIED

157. 5X GREAT-GRANDMOTHER

NAME

BORN

DIED

158. 5X GREAT-GRANDFATHER

NAME

BORN

DIED

MARRIED

NOTES

159. 5X GREAT-GRANDMOTHER

NAME

BORN

DIED

NOTES

160 - 167
5X GREAT-GRANDPARENTS

160. 5X GREAT-GRANDFATHER

NAME

BORN

DIED

MARRIED

161. 5X GREAT-GRANDMOTHER

NAME

BORN

DIED

162. 5X GREAT-GRANDFATHER

NAME

BORN

DIED

MARRIED

NOTES

163. 5X GREAT-GRANDMOTHER

NAME

BORN

DIED

NOTES

164. 5X GREAT-GRANDFATHER

NAME

BORN

DIED

MARRIED

165. 5X GREAT-GRANDMOTHER

NAME

BORN

DIED

166. 5X GREAT-GRANDFATHER

NAME

BORN

DIED

MARRIED

NOTES

167. 5X GREAT-GRANDMOTHER

NAME

BORN

DIED

NOTES

168 – 175
5X GREAT-GRANDPARENTS

168. 5X GREAT-GRANDFATHER

NAME

BORN

DIED

MARRIED

169. 5X GREAT-GRANDMOTHER

NAME

BORN

DIED

170. 5X GREAT-GRANDFATHER

NAME

BORN

DIED

MARRIED

NOTES

171. 5X GREAT-GRANDMOTHER

NAME

BORN

DIED

NOTES

172. 5X GREAT-GRANDFATHER

NAME

BORN

DIED

MARRIED

173. 5X GREAT-GRANDMOTHER

NAME

BORN

DIED

174. 5X GREAT-GRANDFATHER

NAME

BORN

DIED

MARRIED

NOTES

175. 5X GREAT-GRANDMOTHER

NAME

BORN

DIED

NOTES

176 - 183
5X GREAT-GRANDPARENTS

176. 5X GREAT-GRANDFATHER

NAME

BORN

DIED

MARRIED

177. 5X GREAT-GRANDMOTHER

NAME

BORN

DIED

178. 5X GREAT-GRANDFATHER

NAME

BORN

DIED

MARRIED

NOTES

179. 5X GREAT-GRANDMOTHER

NAME

BORN

DIED

NOTES

180. 5X GREAT-GRANDFATHER

NAME

BORN

DIED

MARRIED

181. 5X GREAT-GRANDMOTHER

NAME

BORN

DIED

182. 5X GREAT-GRANDFATHER

NAME

BORN

DIED

MARRIED

NOTES

183. 5X GREAT-GRANDMOTHER

NAME

BORN

DIED

NOTES

184 - 191
5X GREAT-GRANDPARENTS

184. 5X GREAT-GRANDFATHER
NAME

BORN

DIED

MARRIED

185. 5X GREAT-GRANDMOTHER
NAME

BORN

DIED

186. 5X GREAT-GRANDFATHER
NAME

BORN

DIED

MARRIED

NOTES

187. 5X GREAT-GRANDMOTHER
NAME

BORN

DIED

NOTES

188. 5X GREAT-GRANDFATHER
NAME

BORN

DIED

MARRIED

189. 5X GREAT-GRANDMOTHER
NAME

BORN

DIED

190. 5X GREAT-GRANDFATHER
NAME

BORN

DIED

MARRIED

NOTES

191. 5X GREAT-GRANDMOTHER
NAME

BORN

DIED

NOTES

192 - 199
5X GREAT-GRANDPARENTS

192. 5X GREAT-GRANDFATHER
NAME

BORN

DIED

MARRIED

193. 5X GREAT-GRANDMOTHER
NAME

BORN

DIED

194. 5X GREAT-GRANDFATHER
NAME

BORN

DIED

MARRIED

NOTES

195. 5X GREAT-GRANDMOTHER
NAME

BORN

DIED

NOTES

196. 5X GREAT-GRANDFATHER
NAME

BORN

DIED

MARRIED

197. 5X GREAT-GRANDMOTHER
NAME

BORN

DIED

198. 5X GREAT-GRANDFATHER
NAME

BORN

DIED

MARRIED

NOTES

199. 5X GREAT-GRANDMOTHER
NAME

BORN

DIED

NOTES

200 – 207
5X GREAT-GRANDPARENTS

200. 5X GREAT-GRANDFATHER

NAME

BORN

DIED

MARRIED

201. 5X GREAT-GRANDMOTHER

NAME

BORN

DIED

202. 5X GREAT-GRANDFATHER

NAME

BORN

DIED

MARRIED

NOTES

203. 5X GREAT-GRANDMOTHER

NAME

BORN

DIED

NOTES

204. 5X GREAT-GRANDFATHER

NAME

BORN

DIED

MARRIED

205. 5X GREAT-GRANDMOTHER

NAME

BORN

DIED

206. 5X GREAT-GRANDFATHER

NAME

BORN

DIED

MARRIED

NOTES

207. 5X GREAT-GRANDMOTHER

NAME

BORN

DIED

NOTES

208 – 215
5X GREAT-GRANDPARENTS

208. 5X GREAT-GRANDFATHER

NAME

BORN

DIED

MARRIED

209. 5X GREAT-GRANDMOTHER

NAME

BORN

DIED

210. 5X GREAT-GRANDFATHER

NAME

BORN

DIED

MARRIED

NOTES

211. 5X GREAT-GRANDMOTHER

NAME

BORN

DIED

NOTES

212. 5X GREAT-GRANDFATHER

NAME

BORN

DIED

MARRIED

213. 5X GREAT-GRANDMOTHER

NAME

BORN

DIED

214. 5X GREAT-GRANDFATHER

NAME

BORN

DIED

MARRIED

NOTES

215. 5X GREAT-GRANDMOTHER

NAME

BORN

DIED

NOTES

216 – 223
5X GREAT-GRANDPARENTS

216. 5X GREAT-GRANDFATHER
NAME

BORN

DIED

MARRIED

217. 5X GREAT-GRANDMOTHER
NAME

BORN

DIED

218. 5X GREAT-GRANDFATHER
NAME

BORN

DIED

MARRIED

NOTES

219. 5X GREAT-GRANDMOTHER
NAME

BORN

DIED

NOTES

220. 5X GREAT-GRANDFATHER
NAME

BORN

DIED

MARRIED

221. 5X GREAT-GRANDMOTHER
NAME

BORN

DIED

222. 5X GREAT-GRANDFATHER
NAME

BORN

DIED

MARRIED

NOTES

223. 5X GREAT-GRANDMOTHER
NAME

BORN

DIED

NOTES

224 - 231
5X GREAT-GRANDPARENTS

224. 5X GREAT-GRANDFATHER

NAME

BORN

DIED

MARRIED

225. 5X GREAT-GRANDMOTHER

NAME

BORN

DIED

226. 5X GREAT-GRANDFATHER

NAME

BORN

DIED

MARRIED

NOTES

227. 5X GREAT-GRANDMOTHER

NAME

BORN

DIED

NOTES

228. 5X GREAT-GRANDFATHER

NAME

BORN

DIED

MARRIED

229. 5X GREAT-GRANDMOTHER

NAME

BORN

DIED

230. 5X GREAT-GRANDFATHER

NAME

BORN

DIED

MARRIED

NOTES

231. 5X GREAT-GRANDMOTHER

NAME

BORN

DIED

NOTES

232 – 239
5X GREAT-GRANDPARENTS

232. 5X GREAT-GRANDFATHER
NAME

BORN

DIED

MARRIED

233. 5X GREAT-GRANDMOTHER
NAME

BORN

DIED

234. 5X GREAT-GRANDFATHER
NAME

BORN

DIED

MARRIED

NOTES

235. 5X GREAT-GRANDMOTHER
NAME

BORN

DIED

NOTES

236. 5X GREAT-GRANDFATHER
NAME

BORN

DIED

MARRIED

237. 5X GREAT-GRANDMOTHER
NAME

BORN

DIED

238. 5X GREAT-GRANDFATHER
NAME

BORN

DIED

MARRIED

NOTES

239. 5X GREAT-GRANDMOTHER
NAME

BORN

DIED

NOTES

240 - 247
5X GREAT-GRANDPARENTS

240. 5X GREAT-GRANDFATHER
NAME

BORN

DIED

MARRIED

241. 5X GREAT-GRANDMOTHER
NAME

BORN

DIED

242. 5X GREAT-GRANDFATHER
NAME

BORN

DIED

MARRIED

NOTES

243. 5X GREAT-GRANDMOTHER
NAME

BORN

DIED

NOTES

244. 5X GREAT-GRANDFATHER
NAME

BORN

DIED

MARRIED

245. 5X GREAT-GRANDMOTHER
NAME

BORN

DIED

246. 5X GREAT-GRANDFATHER
NAME

BORN

DIED

MARRIED

NOTES

247. 5X GREAT-GRANDMOTHER
NAME

BORN

DIED

NOTES

248 - 255
5X GREAT-GRANDPARENTS

248. 5X GREAT-GRANDFATHER
NAME

BORN

DIED

MARRIED

249. 5X GREAT-GRANDMOTHER
NAME

BORN

DIED

250. 5X GREAT-GRANDFATHER
NAME

BORN

DIED

MARRIED

NOTES

251. 5X GREAT-GRANDMOTHER
NAME

BORN

DIED

NOTES

252. 5X GREAT-GRANDFATHER
NAME

BORN

DIED

MARRIED

253. 5X GREAT-GRANDMOTHER
NAME

BORN

DIED

254. 5X GREAT-GRANDFATHER
NAME

BORN

DIED

MARRIED

NOTES

255. 5X GREAT-GRANDMOTHER
NAME

BORN

DIED

NOTES

THE
9th-12th
GENERATIONS
6X - 9X GREAT-GRANDPARENTS

9th GENERATION: 6X GREAT-GRANDPARENTS

HISTORIC EVENTS THIS GENERATION EXPERIENCED:

10th GENERATION: 7X GREAT-GRANDPARENTS

HISTORIC EVENTS THIS GENERATION EXPERIENCED:

11th GENERATION: 8X GREAT-GRANDPARENTS

HISTORIC EVENTS THIS GENERATION EXPERIENCED:

12th GENERATION: 9X GREAT-GRANDPARENTS

HISTORIC EVENTS THIS GENERATION EXPERIENCED:

THIS CHART STARTS WITH THE PARENTS OF 128.

9th GENERATION	10th GENERATION	11th GENERATION	12th GENERATION
THEIR FATHER	NAME	NAME	NAME
NAME	BORN	BORN	LIVED
BORN	DIED	DIED	NAME
DIED	MARRIED	MARRIED	LIVED
MARRIED	NOTES	NAME	NAME
NOTES		BORN	LIVED
		DIED	NAME
		NOTES	LIVED
	NAME	NAME	NAME
	BORN	BORN	LIVED
	DIED	DIED	NAME
	NOTES	MARRIED	LIVED
		NAME	NAME
		BORN	LIVED
		DIED	NAME
		NOTES	LIVED
THEIR MOTHER	NAME	NAME	NAME
NAME	BORN	BORN	LIVED
BORN	DIED	DIED	NAME
DIED	MARRIED	MARRIED	LIVED
NOTES	NOTES	NAME	NAME
		BORN	LIVED
		DIED	NAME
		NOTES	LIVED
	NAME	NAME	NAME
	BORN	BORN	LIVED
	DIED	DIED	NAME
	NOTES	MARRIED	LIVED
		NAME	NAME
		BORN	LIVED
		DIED	NAME
		NOTES	LIVED

6X GREAT-GRANDPARENTS	7X GREAT-GRANDPARENTS	8X GREAT-GRANDPARENTS	9X GREAT-GRANDPARENTS

*Start by recording the father and mother of the person whose number is listed at the top of this page. Then continue recording the last three generations of their parents, with fathers listed first.

THIS CHART STARTS WITH THE PARENTS OF 129.

9th GENERATION	10th GENERATION	11th GENERATION	12th GENERATION
THEIR FATHER	NAME	NAME	NAME
NAME	BORN	BORN	LIVED
BORN	DIED	DIED	NAME
DIED	MARRIED	MARRIED	LIVED
MARRIED	NOTES	NAME	NAME
NOTES		BORN	LIVED
		DIED	NAME
		NOTES	LIVED
	NAME	NAME	NAME
	BORN	BORN	LIVED
	DIED	DIED	NAME
	NOTES	MARRIED	LIVED
		NAME	NAME
		BORN	LIVED
		DIED	NAME
		NOTES	LIVED
THEIR MOTHER	NAME	NAME	NAME
NAME	BORN	BORN	LIVED
BORN	DIED	DIED	NAME
DIED	MARRIED	MARRIED	LIVED
NOTES	NOTES	NAME	NAME
		BORN	LIVED
		DIED	NAME
		NOTES	LIVED
	NAME	NAME	NAME
	BORN	BORN	LIVED
	DIED	DIED	NAME
	NOTES	MARRIED	LIVED
		NAME	NAME
		BORN	LIVED
		DIED	NAME
		NOTES	LIVED

| 6X GREAT-GRANDPARENTS | 7X GREAT-GRANDPARENTS | 8X GREAT-GRANDPARENTS | 9X GREAT-GRANDPARENTS |

THIS CHART STARTS WITH THE PARENTS OF 130.

9th GENERATION	10th GENERATION	11th GENERATION	12th GENERATION
THEIR FATHER	NAME	NAME	NAME
NAME	BORN	BORN	LIVED
BORN	DIED	DIED	NAME
DIED	MARRIED	MARRIED	LIVED
MARRIED	NOTES	NAME	NAME
NOTES		BORN	LIVED
		DIED	NAME
		NOTES	LIVED
	NAME	NAME	NAME
	BORN	BORN	LIVED
	DIED	DIED	NAME
	NOTES	MARRIED	LIVED
		NAME	NAME
		BORN	LIVED
		DIED	NAME
		NOTES	LIVED
THEIR MOTHER	NAME	NAME	NAME
NAME	BORN	BORN	LIVED
BORN	DIED	DIED	NAME
DIED	MARRIED	MARRIED	LIVED
NOTES	NOTES	NAME	NAME
		BORN	LIVED
		DIED	NAME
		NOTES	LIVED
	NAME	NAME	NAME
	BORN	BORN	LIVED
	DIED	DIED	NAME
	NOTES	MARRIED	LIVED
		NAME	NAME
		BORN	LIVED
		DIED	NAME
		NOTES	LIVED

| 6X GREAT-GRANDPARENTS | 7X GREAT-GRANDPARENTS | 8X GREAT-GRANDPARENTS | 9X GREAT-GRANDPARENTS |

THIS CHART STARTS WITH THE PARENTS OF 131.

9th GENERATION	10th GENERATION	11th GENERATION	12th GENERATION
THEIR FATHER	NAME	NAME	NAME
NAME	BORN	BORN	LIVED
BORN	DIED	DIED	NAME
DIED	MARRIED	MARRIED	LIVED
MARRIED	NOTES	NAME	NAME
NOTES		BORN	LIVED
		DIED	NAME
		NOTES	LIVED
	NAME	NAME	NAME
	BORN	BORN	LIVED
	DIED	DIED	NAME
	NOTES	MARRIED	LIVED
		NAME	NAME
		BORN	LIVED
		DIED	NAME
		NOTES	LIVED
THEIR MOTHER	NAME	NAME	NAME
NAME	BORN	BORN	LIVED
BORN	DIED	DIED	NAME
DIED	MARRIED	MARRIED	LIVED
NOTES	NOTES	NAME	NAME
		BORN	LIVED
		DIED	NAME
		NOTES	LIVED
	NAME	NAME	NAME
	BORN	BORN	LIVED
	DIED	DIED	NAME
	NOTES	MARRIED	LIVED
		NAME	NAME
		BORN	LIVED
		DIED	NAME
		NOTES	LIVED

6X GREAT-GRANDPARENTS	7X GREAT-GRANDPARENTS	8X GREAT-GRANDPARENTS	9X GREAT-GRANDPARENTS

THIS CHART STARTS WITH THE PARENTS OF 132.

9th GENERATION	10th GENERATION	11th GENERATION	12th GENERATION
THEIR FATHER	NAME	NAME	NAME
NAME	BORN	BORN	LIVED
BORN	DIED	DIED	NAME
DIED	MARRIED	MARRIED	LIVED
MARRIED	NOTES	NAME	NAME
NOTES		BORN	LIVED
		DIED	NAME
		NOTES	LIVED
	NAME	NAME	NAME
	BORN	BORN	LIVED
	DIED	DIED	NAME
	NOTES	MARRIED	LIVED
		NAME	NAME
		BORN	LIVED
		DIED	NAME
		NOTES	LIVED
THEIR MOTHER	NAME	NAME	NAME
NAME	BORN	BORN	LIVED
BORN	DIED	DIED	NAME
DIED	MARRIED	MARRIED	LIVED
NOTES	NOTES	NAME	NAME
		BORN	LIVED
		DIED	NAME
		NOTES	LIVED
	NAME	NAME	NAME
	BORN	BORN	LIVED
	DIED	DIED	NAME
	NOTES	MARRIED	LIVED
		NAME	NAME
		BORN	LIVED
		DIED	NAME
		NOTES	LIVED

| 6X GREAT-GRANDPARENTS | 7X GREAT-GRANDPARENTS | 8X GREAT-GRANDPARENTS | 9X GREAT-GRANDPARENTS |

9th GENERATION	10th GENERATION	11th GENERATION	12th GENERATION
THEIR FATHER	NAME	NAME	NAME
NAME	BORN	BORN	LIVED
BORN	DIED	DIED	NAME
DIED	MARRIED	MARRIED	LIVED
MARRIED	NOTES	NAME	NAME
NOTES		BORN	LIVED
		DIED	NAME
		NOTES	LIVED
	NAME	NAME	NAME
	BORN	BORN	LIVED
	DIED	DIED	NAME
	NOTES	MARRIED	LIVED
		NAME	NAME
		BORN	LIVED
		DIED	NAME
		NOTES	LIVED
THEIR MOTHER	NAME	NAME	NAME
NAME	BORN	BORN	LIVED
BORN	DIED	DIED	NAME
DIED	MARRIED	MARRIED	LIVED
NOTES	NOTES	NAME	NAME
		BORN	LIVED
		DIED	NAME
		NOTES	LIVED
	NAME	NAME	NAME
	BORN	BORN	LIVED
	DIED	DIED	NAME
	NOTES	MARRIED	LIVED
		NAME	NAME
		BORN	LIVED
		DIED	NAME
		NOTES	LIVED

6X GREAT-GRANDPARENTS	7X GREAT-GRANDPARENTS	8X GREAT-GRANDPARENTS	9X GREAT-GRANDPARENTS

THIS CHART STARTS WITH THE PARENTS OF 134.

9th GENERATION	10th GENERATION	11th GENERATION	12th GENERATION
THEIR FATHER	NAME	NAME	NAME
NAME	BORN	BORN	LIVED
BORN	DIED	DIED	NAME
DIED	MARRIED	MARRIED	LIVED
MARRIED	NOTES	NAME	NAME
NOTES		BORN	LIVED
		DIED	NAME
		NOTES	LIVED
			NAME
			LIVED
	NAME	NAME	NAME
	BORN	BORN	LIVED
	DIED	DIED	NAME
	NOTES	MARRIED	LIVED
		NAME	NAME
		BORN	LIVED
		DIED	NAME
		NOTES	LIVED
THEIR MOTHER	NAME	NAME	NAME
NAME	BORN	BORN	LIVED
BORN	DIED	DIED	NAME
DIED	MARRIED	MARRIED	LIVED
NOTES	NOTES	NAME	NAME
		BORN	LIVED
		DIED	NAME
		NOTES	LIVED
	NAME	NAME	NAME
	BORN	BORN	LIVED
	DIED	DIED	NAME
	NOTES	MARRIED	LIVED
		NAME	NAME
		BORN	LIVED
		DIED	NAME
		NOTES	LIVED

6X GREAT-GRANDPARENTS	7X GREAT-GRANDPARENTS	8X GREAT-GRANDPARENTS	9X GREAT-GRANDPARENTS

THIS CHART STARTS WITH THE PARENTS OF 135.

9th GENERATION	10th GENERATION	11th GENERATION	12th GENERATION
THEIR FATHER	NAME	NAME	NAME
			LIVED
NAME	BORN	BORN	
			NAME
BORN	DIED	DIED	LIVED
DIED	MARRIED	MARRIED	NAME
			LIVED
MARRIED	NOTES	NAME	
			NAME
NOTES		BORN	LIVED
		DIED	NAME
			LIVED
		NOTES	
			NAME
			LIVED
	NAME	NAME	
			NAME
	BORN	BORN	LIVED
	DIED	DIED	NAME
			LIVED
	NOTES	MARRIED	
			NAME
		NAME	LIVED
		BORN	NAME
			LIVED
		DIED	
			NAME
		NOTES	LIVED
THEIR MOTHER	NAME	NAME	NAME
			LIVED
NAME	BORN	BORN	
			NAME
BORN	DIED	DIED	LIVED
DIED	MARRIED	MARRIED	NAME
			LIVED
NOTES	NOTES	NAME	
			NAME
		BORN	LIVED
		DIED	NAME
			LIVED
		NOTES	
			NAME
			LIVED
	NAME	NAME	
			NAME
	BORN	BORN	LIVED
	DIED	DIED	NAME
			LIVED
	NOTES	MARRIED	
			NAME
		NAME	LIVED
		BORN	NAME
			LIVED
		DIED	
			NAME
		NOTES	LIVED

| 6X GREAT-GRANDPARENTS | 7X GREAT-GRANDPARENTS | 8X GREAT-GRANDPARENTS | 9X GREAT-GRANDPARENTS |

THIS CHART STARTS WITH THE PARENTS OF 136.

9th GENERATION	10th GENERATION	11th GENERATION	12th GENERATION
THEIR FATHER	NAME	NAME	NAME
NAME	BORN	BORN	LIVED
BORN	DIED	DIED	NAME
DIED	MARRIED	MARRIED	LIVED
MARRIED	NOTES	NAME	NAME
NOTES		BORN	LIVED
		DIED	NAME
		NOTES	LIVED
	NAME	NAME	NAME
	BORN	BORN	LIVED
	DIED	DIED	NAME
	NOTES	MARRIED	LIVED
		NAME	NAME
		BORN	LIVED
		DIED	NAME
		NOTES	LIVED
THEIR MOTHER	NAME	NAME	NAME
NAME	BORN	BORN	LIVED
BORN	DIED	DIED	NAME
DIED	MARRIED	MARRIED	LIVED
NOTES	NOTES	NAME	NAME
		BORN	LIVED
		DIED	NAME
		NOTES	LIVED
	NAME	NAME	NAME
	BORN	BORN	LIVED
	DIED	DIED	NAME
	NOTES	MARRIED	LIVED
		NAME	NAME
		BORN	LIVED
		DIED	NAME
		NOTES	LIVED

6X GREAT-GRANDPARENTS	7X GREAT-GRANDPARENTS	8X GREAT-GRANDPARENTS	9X GREAT-GRANDPARENTS

9th GENERATION	10th GENERATION	11th GENERATION	12th GENERATION
THEIR FATHER	NAME	NAME	NAME
NAME	BORN	BORN	LIVED
BORN	DIED	DIED	NAME
DIED	MARRIED	MARRIED	LIVED
MARRIED	NOTES	NAME	NAME
NOTES		BORN	LIVED
		DIED	NAME
		NOTES	LIVED
	NAME	NAME	NAME
	BORN	BORN	LIVED
	DIED	DIED	NAME
	NOTES	MARRIED	LIVED
		NAME	NAME
		BORN	LIVED
		DIED	NAME
		NOTES	LIVED
THEIR MOTHER	NAME	NAME	NAME
NAME	BORN	BORN	LIVED
BORN	DIED	DIED	NAME
DIED	MARRIED	MARRIED	LIVED
NOTES	NOTES	NAME	NAME
		BORN	LIVED
		DIED	NAME
		NOTES	LIVED
	NAME	NAME	NAME
	BORN	BORN	LIVED
	DIED	DIED	NAME
	NOTES	MARRIED	LIVED
		NAME	NAME
		BORN	LIVED
		DIED	NAME
		NOTES	LIVED

6X GREAT-GRANDPARENTS	7X GREAT-GRANDPARENTS	8X GREAT-GRANDPARENTS	9X GREAT-GRANDPARENTS

THIS CHART STARTS WITH THE PARENTS OF 138.

9th GENERATION	10th GENERATION	11th GENERATION	12th GENERATION
THEIR FATHER	NAME	NAME	NAME
NAME	BORN	BORN	LIVED
BORN	DIED	DIED	NAME
DIED	MARRIED	MARRIED	LIVED
MARRIED	NOTES	NAME	NAME
NOTES		BORN	LIVED
		DIED	NAME
		NOTES	LIVED
	NAME	NAME	NAME
	BORN	BORN	LIVED
	DIED	DIED	NAME
	NOTES	MARRIED	LIVED
		NAME	NAME
		BORN	LIVED
		DIED	NAME
		NOTES	LIVED
THEIR MOTHER	NAME	NAME	NAME
NAME	BORN	BORN	LIVED
BORN	DIED	DIED	NAME
DIED	MARRIED	MARRIED	LIVED
NOTES	NOTES	NAME	NAME
		BORN	LIVED
		DIED	NAME
		NOTES	LIVED
	NAME	NAME	NAME
	BORN	BORN	LIVED
	DIED	DIED	NAME
	NOTES	MARRIED	LIVED
		NAME	NAME
		BORN	LIVED
		DIED	NAME
		NOTES	LIVED

| 6X GREAT-GRANDPARENTS | 7X GREAT-GRANDPARENTS | 8X GREAT-GRANDPARENTS | 9X GREAT-GRANDPARENTS |

THIS CHART STARTS WITH THE PARENTS OF 139.

9th GENERATION	10th GENERATION	11th GENERATION	12th GENERATION
THEIR FATHER	NAME	NAME	NAME
NAME	BORN	BORN	LIVED
BORN	DIED	DIED	NAME
DIED	MARRIED	MARRIED	LIVED
MARRIED	NOTES	NAME	NAME
NOTES		BORN	LIVED
		DIED	NAME
		NOTES	LIVED
	NAME	NAME	NAME
	BORN	BORN	LIVED
	DIED	DIED	NAME
	NOTES	MARRIED	LIVED
		NAME	NAME
		BORN	LIVED
		DIED	NAME
		NOTES	LIVED
THEIR MOTHER	NAME	NAME	NAME
NAME	BORN	BORN	LIVED
BORN	DIED	DIED	NAME
DIED	MARRIED	MARRIED	LIVED
NOTES	NOTES	NAME	NAME
		BORN	LIVED
		DIED	NAME
		NOTES	LIVED
	NAME	NAME	NAME
	BORN	BORN	LIVED
	DIED	DIED	NAME
	NOTES	MARRIED	LIVED
		NAME	NAME
		BORN	LIVED
		DIED	NAME
		NOTES	LIVED

| 6X GREAT-GRANDPARENTS | 7X GREAT-GRANDPARENTS | 8X GREAT-GRANDPARENTS | 9X GREAT-GRANDPARENTS |

THIS CHART STARTS WITH THE PARENTS OF 140.

9th GENERATION	10th GENERATION	11th GENERATION	12th GENERATION
THEIR FATHER	NAME	NAME	NAME
NAME	BORN	BORN	LIVED
BORN	DIED	DIED	NAME
DIED	MARRIED	MARRIED	LIVED
MARRIED	NOTES	NAME	NAME
NOTES		BORN	LIVED
		DIED	NAME
		NOTES	LIVED
	NAME	NAME	NAME
	BORN	BORN	LIVED
	DIED	DIED	NAME
	NOTES	MARRIED	LIVED
		NAME	NAME
		BORN	LIVED
		DIED	NAME
		NOTES	LIVED
THEIR MOTHER	NAME	NAME	NAME
NAME	BORN	BORN	LIVED
BORN	DIED	DIED	NAME
DIED	MARRIED	MARRIED	LIVED
NOTES	NOTES	NAME	NAME
		BORN	LIVED
		DIED	NAME
		NOTES	LIVED
	NAME	NAME	NAME
	BORN	BORN	LIVED
	DIED	DIED	NAME
	NOTES	MARRIED	LIVED
		NAME	NAME
		BORN	LIVED
		DIED	NAME
		NOTES	LIVED

6X GREAT-GRANDPARENTS	7X GREAT-GRANDPARENTS	8X GREAT-GRANDPARENTS	9X GREAT-GRANDPARENTS

THIS CHART STARTS WITH THE PARENTS OF 141.

9th GENERATION	10th GENERATION	11th GENERATION	12th GENERATION
THEIR FATHER	NAME	NAME	NAME
NAME	BORN	BORN	LIVED
BORN	DIED	DIED	NAME
DIED	MARRIED	MARRIED	LIVED
MARRIED	NOTES	NAME	NAME
NOTES		BORN	LIVED
		DIED	NAME
		NOTES	LIVED
	NAME	NAME	NAME
	BORN	BORN	LIVED
	DIED	DIED	NAME
	NOTES	MARRIED	LIVED
		NAME	NAME
		BORN	LIVED
		DIED	NAME
		NOTES	LIVED
THEIR MOTHER	NAME	NAME	NAME
NAME	BORN	BORN	LIVED
BORN	DIED	DIED	NAME
DIED	MARRIED	MARRIED	LIVED
NOTES	NOTES	NAME	NAME
		BORN	LIVED
		DIED	NAME
		NOTES	LIVED
	NAME	NAME	NAME
	BORN	BORN	LIVED
	DIED	DIED	NAME
	NOTES	MARRIED	LIVED
		NAME	NAME
		BORN	LIVED
		DIED	NAME
		NOTES	LIVED

6X GREAT-GRANDPARENTS	7X GREAT-GRANDPARENTS	8X GREAT-GRANDPARENTS	9X GREAT-GRANDPARENTS

THIS CHART STARTS WITH THE PARENTS OF 142.

9th GENERATION	10th GENERATION	11th GENERATION	12th GENERATION
THEIR FATHER NAME BORN DIED MARRIED NOTES	NAME BORN DIED MARRIED NOTES	NAME BORN DIED MARRIED	NAME LIVED
			NAME LIVED
		NAME BORN DIED NOTES	NAME LIVED
			NAME LIVED
			NAME LIVED
	NAME BORN DIED NOTES	NAME BORN DIED MARRIED	NAME LIVED
			NAME LIVED
		NAME BORN DIED NOTES	NAME LIVED
			NAME LIVED
			NAME LIVED
THEIR MOTHER NAME BORN DIED NOTES	NAME BORN DIED MARRIED NOTES	NAME BORN DIED MARRIED	NAME LIVED
			NAME LIVED
		NAME BORN DIED NOTES	NAME LIVED
			NAME LIVED
			NAME LIVED
	NAME BORN DIED NOTES	NAME BORN DIED MARRIED	NAME LIVED
			NAME LIVED
		NAME BORN DIED NOTES	NAME LIVED
			NAME LIVED
			NAME LIVED

| 6X GREAT-GRANDPARENTS | 7X GREAT-GRANDPARENTS | 8X GREAT-GRANDPARENTS | 9X GREAT-GRANDPARENTS |

THIS CHART STARTS WITH THE PARENTS OF 143.

9th GENERATION	10th GENERATION	11th GENERATION	12th GENERATION
THEIR FATHER	NAME	NAME	NAME
NAME	BORN	BORN	LIVED
BORN	DIED	DIED	NAME
DIED	MARRIED	MARRIED	LIVED
MARRIED	NOTES	NAME	NAME
NOTES		BORN	LIVED
		DIED	NAME
		NOTES	LIVED
	NAME	NAME	NAME
	BORN	BORN	LIVED
	DIED	DIED	NAME
	NOTES	MARRIED	LIVED
		NAME	NAME
		BORN	LIVED
		DIED	NAME
		NOTES	LIVED
THEIR MOTHER	NAME	NAME	NAME
NAME	BORN	BORN	LIVED
BORN	DIED	DIED	NAME
DIED	MARRIED	MARRIED	LIVED
NOTES	NOTES	NAME	NAME
		BORN	LIVED
		DIED	NAME
		NOTES	LIVED
	NAME	NAME	NAME
	BORN	BORN	LIVED
	DIED	DIED	NAME
	NOTES	MARRIED	LIVED
		NAME	NAME
		BORN	LIVED
		DIED	NAME
		NOTES	LIVED

| 6X GREAT-GRANDPARENTS | 7X GREAT-GRANDPARENTS | 8X GREAT-GRANDPARENTS | 9X GREAT-GRANDPARENTS |

THIS CHART STARTS WITH THE PARENTS OF 144.

9th GENERATION	10th GENERATION	11th GENERATION	12th GENERATION
THEIR FATHER NAME BORN DIED MARRIED NOTES	NAME BORN DIED MARRIED NOTES	NAME BORN DIED MARRIED	NAME LIVED
			NAME LIVED
		NAME BORN DIED NOTES	NAME LIVED
			NAME LIVED
			NAME LIVED
	NAME BORN DIED NOTES	NAME BORN DIED MARRIED	NAME LIVED
			NAME LIVED
		NAME BORN DIED NOTES	NAME LIVED
			NAME LIVED
THEIR MOTHER NAME BORN DIED NOTES	NAME BORN DIED MARRIED NOTES	NAME BORN DIED MARRIED	NAME LIVED
			NAME LIVED
		NAME BORN DIED NOTES	NAME LIVED
			NAME LIVED
	NAME BORN DIED NOTES	NAME BORN DIED MARRIED	NAME LIVED
			NAME LIVED
		NAME BORN DIED NOTES	NAME LIVED
			NAME LIVED

6X GREAT-GRANDPARENTS	7X GREAT-GRANDPARENTS	8X GREAT-GRANDPARENTS	9X GREAT-GRANDPARENTS

THIS CHART STARTS WITH THE PARENTS OF 145.

9th GENERATION	10th GENERATION	11th GENERATION	12th GENERATION
THEIR FATHER	NAME	NAME	NAME
NAME	BORN	BORN	LIVED
BORN	DIED	DIED	NAME
DIED	MARRIED	MARRIED	LIVED
MARRIED	NOTES	NAME	NAME
NOTES		BORN	LIVED
		DIED	NAME
		NOTES	LIVED
	NAME	NAME	NAME
	BORN	BORN	LIVED
	DIED	DIED	NAME
	NOTES	MARRIED	LIVED
		NAME	NAME
		BORN	LIVED
		DIED	NAME
		NOTES	LIVED
THEIR MOTHER	NAME	NAME	NAME
NAME	BORN	BORN	LIVED
BORN	DIED	DIED	NAME
DIED	MARRIED	MARRIED	LIVED
NOTES	NOTES	NAME	NAME
		BORN	LIVED
		DIED	NAME
		NOTES	LIVED
	NAME	NAME	NAME
	BORN	BORN	LIVED
	DIED	DIED	NAME
	NOTES	MARRIED	LIVED
		NAME	NAME
		BORN	LIVED
		DIED	NAME
		NOTES	LIVED

| 6X GREAT-GRANDPARENTS | 7X GREAT-GRANDPARENTS | 8X GREAT-GRANDPARENTS | 9X GREAT-GRANDPARENTS |

THIS CHART STARTS WITH THE PARENTS OF 146.

9th GENERATION	10th GENERATION	11th GENERATION	12th GENERATION
THEIR FATHER NAME BORN DIED MARRIED NOTES	NAME BORN DIED MARRIED NOTES	NAME BORN DIED MARRIED	NAME LIVED
			NAME LIVED
		NAME BORN DIED NOTES	NAME LIVED
			NAME LIVED
	NAME BORN DIED NOTES	NAME BORN DIED MARRIED	NAME LIVED
			NAME LIVED
		NAME BORN DIED NOTES	NAME LIVED
			NAME LIVED
THEIR MOTHER NAME BORN DIED NOTES	NAME BORN DIED MARRIED NOTES	NAME BORN DIED MARRIED	NAME LIVED
			NAME LIVED
		NAME BORN DIED NOTES	NAME LIVED
			NAME LIVED
	NAME BORN DIED NOTES	NAME BORN DIED MARRIED	NAME LIVED
			NAME LIVED
		NAME BORN DIED NOTES	NAME LIVED
			NAME LIVED

| 6X GREAT-GRANDPARENTS | 7X GREAT-GRANDPARENTS | 8X GREAT-GRANDPARENTS | 9X GREAT-GRANDPARENTS |

9th GENERATION	10th GENERATION	11th GENERATION	12th GENERATION
THEIR FATHER	NAME	NAME	NAME
NAME	BORN	BORN	LIVED
BORN	DIED	DIED	NAME
DIED	MARRIED	MARRIED	LIVED
MARRIED	NOTES	NAME	NAME
NOTES		BORN	LIVED
		DIED	NAME
		NOTES	LIVED
	NAME	NAME	NAME
	BORN	BORN	LIVED
	DIED	DIED	NAME
	NOTES	MARRIED	LIVED
		NAME	NAME
		BORN	LIVED
		DIED	NAME
		NOTES	LIVED
THEIR MOTHER	NAME	NAME	NAME
NAME	BORN	BORN	LIVED
BORN	DIED	DIED	NAME
DIED	MARRIED	MARRIED	LIVED
NOTES	NOTES	NAME	NAME
		BORN	LIVED
		DIED	NAME
		NOTES	LIVED
	NAME	NAME	NAME
	BORN	BORN	LIVED
	DIED	DIED	NAME
	NOTES	MARRIED	LIVED
		NAME	NAME
		BORN	LIVED
		DIED	NAME
		NOTES	LIVED

| 6X GREAT-GRANDPARENTS | 7X GREAT-GRANDPARENTS | 8X GREAT-GRANDPARENTS | 9X GREAT-GRANDPARENTS |

THIS CHART STARTS WITH THE PARENTS OF 148.

9th GENERATION	10th GENERATION	11th GENERATION	12th GENERATION
THEIR FATHER	NAME	NAME	NAME
NAME	BORN	BORN	LIVED
BORN	DIED	DIED	NAME
DIED	MARRIED	MARRIED	LIVED
MARRIED	NOTES	NAME	NAME
NOTES		BORN	LIVED
		DIED	NAME
		NOTES	LIVED
	NAME	NAME	NAME
	BORN	BORN	LIVED
	DIED	DIED	NAME
	NOTES	MARRIED	LIVED
		NAME	NAME
		BORN	LIVED
		DIED	NAME
		NOTES	LIVED
THEIR MOTHER	NAME	NAME	NAME
NAME	BORN	BORN	LIVED
BORN	DIED	DIED	NAME
DIED	MARRIED	MARRIED	LIVED
NOTES	NOTES	NAME	NAME
		BORN	LIVED
		DIED	NAME
		NOTES	LIVED
	NAME	NAME	NAME
	BORN	BORN	LIVED
	DIED	DIED	NAME
	NOTES	MARRIED	LIVED
		NAME	NAME
		BORN	LIVED
		DIED	NAME
		NOTES	LIVED

| 6X GREAT-GRANDPARENTS | 7X GREAT-GRANDPARENTS | 8X GREAT-GRANDPARENTS | 9X GREAT-GRANDPARENTS |

9th GENERATION	10th GENERATION	11th GENERATION	12th GENERATION
THEIR FATHER	NAME	NAME	NAME
NAME	BORN	BORN	LIVED
BORN	DIED	DIED	NAME
DIED	MARRIED	MARRIED	LIVED
MARRIED	NOTES	NAME	NAME
NOTES		BORN	LIVED
		DIED	NAME
		NOTES	LIVED
	NAME	NAME	NAME
	BORN	BORN	LIVED
	DIED	DIED	NAME
	NOTES	MARRIED	LIVED
		NAME	NAME
		BORN	LIVED
		DIED	NAME
		NOTES	LIVED
THEIR MOTHER	NAME	NAME	NAME
NAME	BORN	BORN	LIVED
BORN	DIED	DIED	NAME
DIED	MARRIED	MARRIED	LIVED
NOTES	NOTES	NAME	NAME
		BORN	LIVED
		DIED	NAME
		NOTES	LIVED
	NAME	NAME	NAME
	BORN	BORN	LIVED
	DIED	DIED	NAME
	NOTES	MARRIED	LIVED
		NAME	NAME
		BORN	LIVED
		DIED	NAME
		NOTES	LIVED

6X GREAT-GRANDPARENTS	7X GREAT-GRANDPARENTS	8X GREAT-GRANDPARENTS	9X GREAT-GRANDPARENTS

THIS CHART STARTS WITH THE PARENTS OF 150.

9th GENERATION	10th GENERATION	11th GENERATION	12th GENERATION
THEIR FATHER	NAME	NAME	NAME
NAME	BORN	BORN	LIVED
BORN	DIED	DIED	NAME
DIED	MARRIED	MARRIED	LIVED
MARRIED	NOTES	NAME	NAME
NOTES		BORN	LIVED
		DIED	NAME
		NOTES	LIVED
	NAME	NAME	NAME
	BORN	BORN	LIVED
	DIED	DIED	NAME
	NOTES	MARRIED	LIVED
		NAME	NAME
		BORN	LIVED
		DIED	NAME
		NOTES	LIVED
THEIR MOTHER	NAME	NAME	NAME
NAME	BORN	BORN	LIVED
BORN	DIED	DIED	NAME
DIED	MARRIED	MARRIED	LIVED
NOTES	NOTES	NAME	NAME
		BORN	LIVED
		DIED	NAME
		NOTES	LIVED
	NAME	NAME	NAME
	BORN	BORN	LIVED
	DIED	DIED	NAME
	NOTES	MARRIED	LIVED
		NAME	NAME
		BORN	LIVED
		DIED	NAME
		NOTES	LIVED

6X GREAT-GRANDPARENTS	7X GREAT-GRANDPARENTS	8X GREAT-GRANDPARENTS	9X GREAT-GRANDPARENTS

THIS CHART STARTS WITH THE PARENTS OF 151.

9th GENERATION	10th GENERATION	11th GENERATION	12th GENERATION
THEIR FATHER	NAME	NAME	NAME
NAME	BORN	BORN	LIVED
BORN	DIED	DIED	NAME
DIED	MARRIED	MARRIED	LIVED
MARRIED	NOTES	NAME	NAME
NOTES		BORN	LIVED
		DIED	NAME
		NOTES	LIVED
	NAME	NAME	NAME
	BORN	BORN	LIVED
	DIED	DIED	NAME
	NOTES	MARRIED	LIVED
		NAME	NAME
		BORN	LIVED
		DIED	NAME
		NOTES	LIVED
THEIR MOTHER	NAME	NAME	NAME
NAME	BORN	BORN	LIVED
BORN	DIED	DIED	NAME
DIED	MARRIED	MARRIED	LIVED
NOTES	NOTES	NAME	NAME
		BORN	LIVED
		DIED	NAME
		NOTES	LIVED
	NAME	NAME	NAME
	BORN	BORN	LIVED
	DIED	DIED	NAME
	NOTES	MARRIED	LIVED
		NAME	NAME
		BORN	LIVED
		DIED	NAME
		NOTES	LIVED
6X GREAT-GRANDPARENTS	7X GREAT-GRANDPARENTS	8X GREAT-GRANDPARENTS	9X GREAT-GRANDPARENTS

THIS CHART STARTS WITH THE PARENTS OF 152.

9th GENERATION	10th GENERATION	11th GENERATION	12th GENERATION
THEIR FATHER	NAME	NAME	NAME
NAME	BORN	BORN	LIVED
BORN	DIED	DIED	NAME
DIED	MARRIED	MARRIED	LIVED
MARRIED	NOTES	NAME	NAME
NOTES		BORN	LIVED
		DIED	NAME
		NOTES	LIVED
	NAME	NAME	NAME
	BORN	BORN	LIVED
	DIED	DIED	NAME
	NOTES	MARRIED	LIVED
		NAME	NAME
		BORN	LIVED
		DIED	NAME
		NOTES	LIVED
THEIR MOTHER	NAME	NAME	NAME
NAME	BORN	BORN	LIVED
BORN	DIED	DIED	NAME
DIED	MARRIED	MARRIED	LIVED
NOTES	NOTES	NAME	NAME
		BORN	LIVED
		DIED	NAME
		NOTES	LIVED
	NAME	NAME	NAME
	BORN	BORN	LIVED
	DIED	DIED	NAME
	NOTES	MARRIED	LIVED
		NAME	NAME
		BORN	LIVED
		DIED	NAME
		NOTES	LIVED

| 6X GREAT-GRANDPARENTS | 7X GREAT-GRANDPARENTS | 8X GREAT-GRANDPARENTS | 9X GREAT-GRANDPARENTS |

THIS CHART STARTS WITH THE PARENTS OF 153.

9th GENERATION	10th GENERATION	11th GENERATION	12th GENERATION
THEIR FATHER	NAME	NAME	NAME
NAME	BORN	BORN	LIVED
BORN	DIED	DIED	NAME
DIED	MARRIED	MARRIED	LIVED
MARRIED	NOTES	NAME	NAME
NOTES		BORN	LIVED
		DIED	NAME
		NOTES	LIVED
	NAME	NAME	NAME
	BORN	BORN	LIVED
	DIED	DIED	NAME
	NOTES	MARRIED	LIVED
		NAME	NAME
		BORN	LIVED
		DIED	NAME
		NOTES	LIVED
THEIR MOTHER	NAME	NAME	NAME
NAME	BORN	BORN	LIVED
BORN	DIED	DIED	NAME
DIED	MARRIED	MARRIED	LIVED
NOTES	NOTES	NAME	NAME
		BORN	LIVED
		DIED	NAME
		NOTES	LIVED
	NAME	NAME	NAME
	BORN	BORN	LIVED
	DIED	DIED	NAME
	NOTES	MARRIED	LIVED
		NAME	NAME
		BORN	LIVED
		DIED	NAME
		NOTES	LIVED

6X GREAT-GRANDPARENTS	7X GREAT-GRANDPARENTS	8X GREAT-GRANDPARENTS	9X GREAT-GRANDPARENTS

THIS CHART STARTS WITH THE PARENTS OF 154.

9th GENERATION	10th GENERATION	11th GENERATION	12th GENERATION
THEIR FATHER NAME BORN DIED MARRIED NOTES	NAME BORN DIED MARRIED NOTES	NAME BORN DIED MARRIED	NAME LIVED
			NAME LIVED
		NAME BORN DIED NOTES	NAME LIVED
			NAME LIVED
	NAME BORN DIED NOTES	NAME BORN DIED MARRIED	NAME LIVED
			NAME LIVED
		NAME BORN DIED NOTES	NAME LIVED
			NAME LIVED
THEIR MOTHER NAME BORN DIED NOTES	NAME BORN DIED MARRIED NOTES	NAME BORN DIED MARRIED	NAME LIVED
			NAME LIVED
		NAME BORN DIED NOTES	NAME LIVED
			NAME LIVED
	NAME BORN DIED NOTES	NAME BORN DIED MARRIED	NAME LIVED
			NAME LIVED
		NAME BORN DIED NOTES	NAME LIVED
			NAME LIVED
6X GREAT-GRANDPARENTS	7X GREAT-GRANDPARENTS	8X GREAT-GRANDPARENTS	9X GREAT-GRANDPARENTS

THIS CHART STARTS WITH THE PARENTS OF 155.

9th GENERATION	10th GENERATION	11th GENERATION	12th GENERATION
THEIR FATHER NAME BORN DIED MARRIED NOTES	NAME BORN DIED MARRIED NOTES	NAME BORN DIED MARRIED	NAME LIVED
			NAME LIVED
		NAME BORN DIED NOTES	NAME LIVED
			NAME LIVED
			NAME LIVED
	NAME BORN DIED NOTES	NAME BORN DIED MARRIED	NAME LIVED
			NAME LIVED
		NAME BORN DIED NOTES	NAME LIVED
			NAME LIVED
THEIR MOTHER NAME BORN DIED NOTES	NAME BORN DIED MARRIED NOTES	NAME BORN DIED MARRIED	NAME LIVED
			NAME LIVED
		NAME BORN DIED NOTES	NAME LIVED
			NAME LIVED
	NAME BORN DIED NOTES	NAME BORN DIED MARRIED	NAME LIVED
			NAME LIVED
		NAME BORN DIED NOTES	NAME LIVED
			NAME LIVED

| 6X GREAT-GRANDPARENTS | 7X GREAT-GRANDPARENTS | 8X GREAT-GRANDPARENTS | 9X GREAT-GRANDPARENTS |

THIS CHART STARTS WITH THE PARENTS OF 156.

9th GENERATION	10th GENERATION	11th GENERATION	12th GENERATION
THEIR FATHER NAME BORN DIED MARRIED NOTES	NAME BORN DIED MARRIED NOTES	NAME BORN DIED MARRIED	NAME LIVED
			NAME LIVED
		NAME BORN DIED NOTES	NAME LIVED
			NAME LIVED
			NAME LIVED
	NAME BORN DIED NOTES	NAME BORN DIED MARRIED	NAME LIVED
			NAME LIVED
		NAME BORN DIED NOTES	NAME LIVED
			NAME LIVED
THEIR MOTHER NAME BORN DIED NOTES	NAME BORN DIED MARRIED NOTES	NAME BORN DIED MARRIED	NAME LIVED
			NAME LIVED
		NAME BORN DIED NOTES	NAME LIVED
			NAME LIVED
			NAME LIVED
	NAME BORN DIED NOTES	NAME BORN DIED MARRIED	NAME LIVED
			NAME LIVED
		NAME BORN DIED NOTES	NAME LIVED
			NAME LIVED

| 6X GREAT-GRANDPARENTS | 7X GREAT-GRANDPARENTS | 8X GREAT-GRANDPARENTS | 9X GREAT-GRANDPARENTS |

9th GENERATION	10th GENERATION	11th GENERATION	12th GENERATION
THEIR FATHER	NAME	NAME	NAME
NAME	BORN	BORN	LIVED
BORN	DIED	DIED	NAME
DIED	MARRIED	MARRIED	LIVED
MARRIED	NOTES	NAME	NAME
NOTES		BORN	LIVED
		DIED	NAME
		NOTES	LIVED
	NAME	NAME	NAME
	BORN	BORN	LIVED
	DIED	DIED	NAME
	NOTES	MARRIED	LIVED
		NAME	NAME
		BORN	LIVED
		DIED	NAME
		NOTES	LIVED
THEIR MOTHER	NAME	NAME	NAME
NAME	BORN	BORN	LIVED
BORN	DIED	DIED	NAME
DIED	MARRIED	MARRIED	LIVED
NOTES	NOTES	NAME	NAME
		BORN	LIVED
		DIED	NAME
		NOTES	LIVED
	NAME	NAME	NAME
	BORN	BORN	LIVED
	DIED	DIED	NAME
	NOTES	MARRIED	LIVED
		NAME	NAME
		BORN	LIVED
		DIED	NAME
		NOTES	LIVED

6X GREAT-GRANDPARENTS	7X GREAT-GRANDPARENTS	8X GREAT-GRANDPARENTS	9X GREAT-GRANDPARENTS

THIS CHART STARTS WITH THE PARENTS OF 158.

9th GENERATION	10th GENERATION	11th GENERATION	12th GENERATION
THEIR FATHER NAME BORN DIED MARRIED NOTES	NAME BORN DIED MARRIED NOTES	NAME BORN DIED MARRIED	NAME LIVED
			NAME LIVED
		NAME BORN DIED NOTES	NAME LIVED
			NAME LIVED
			NAME LIVED
	NAME BORN DIED NOTES	NAME BORN DIED MARRIED	NAME LIVED
			NAME LIVED
		NAME BORN DIED NOTES	NAME LIVED
			NAME LIVED
			NAME LIVED
THEIR MOTHER NAME BORN DIED NOTES	NAME BORN DIED MARRIED NOTES	NAME BORN DIED MARRIED	NAME LIVED
			NAME LIVED
		NAME BORN DIED NOTES	NAME LIVED
			NAME LIVED
			NAME LIVED
	NAME BORN DIED NOTES	NAME BORN DIED MARRIED	NAME LIVED
			NAME LIVED
		NAME BORN DIED NOTES	NAME LIVED
			NAME LIVED
			NAME LIVED

| 6X GREAT-GRANDPARENTS | 7X GREAT-GRANDPARENTS | 8X GREAT-GRANDPARENTS | 9X GREAT-GRANDPARENTS |

THIS CHART STARTS WITH THE PARENTS OF 159.

9th GENERATION	10th GENERATION	11th GENERATION	12th GENERATION
THEIR FATHER	NAME	NAME	NAME
NAME	BORN	BORN	LIVED
BORN	DIED	DIED	NAME
DIED	MARRIED	MARRIED	LIVED
MARRIED	NOTES	NAME	NAME
NOTES		BORN	LIVED
		DIED	NAME
		NOTES	LIVED
	NAME	NAME	NAME
	BORN	BORN	LIVED
	DIED	DIED	NAME
	NOTES	MARRIED	LIVED
		NAME	NAME
		BORN	LIVED
		DIED	NAME
		NOTES	LIVED
THEIR MOTHER	NAME	NAME	NAME
NAME	BORN	BORN	LIVED
BORN	DIED	DIED	NAME
DIED	MARRIED	MARRIED	LIVED
NOTES	NOTES	NAME	NAME
		BORN	LIVED
		DIED	NAME
		NOTES	LIVED
	NAME	NAME	NAME
	BORN	BORN	LIVED
	DIED	DIED	NAME
	NOTES	MARRIED	LIVED
		NAME	NAME
		BORN	LIVED
		DIED	NAME
		NOTES	LIVED

6X GREAT-GRANDPARENTS	7X GREAT-GRANDPARENTS	8X GREAT-GRANDPARENTS	9X GREAT-GRANDPARENTS

THIS CHART STARTS WITH THE PARENTS OF 160.

9th GENERATION	10th GENERATION	11th GENERATION	12th GENERATION
THEIR FATHER	NAME	NAME	NAME
NAME	BORN	BORN	LIVED
BORN	DIED	DIED	NAME
DIED	MARRIED	MARRIED	LIVED
MARRIED	NOTES	NAME	NAME
NOTES		BORN	LIVED
		DIED	NAME
		NOTES	LIVED
	NAME	NAME	NAME
	BORN	BORN	LIVED
	DIED	DIED	NAME
	NOTES	MARRIED	LIVED
		NAME	NAME
		BORN	LIVED
		DIED	NAME
		NOTES	LIVED
THEIR MOTHER	NAME	NAME	NAME
NAME	BORN	BORN	LIVED
BORN	DIED	DIED	NAME
DIED	MARRIED	MARRIED	LIVED
NOTES	NOTES	NAME	NAME
		BORN	LIVED
		DIED	NAME
		NOTES	LIVED
	NAME	NAME	NAME
	BORN	BORN	LIVED
	DIED	DIED	NAME
	NOTES	MARRIED	LIVED
		NAME	NAME
		BORN	LIVED
		DIED	NAME
		NOTES	LIVED

| 6X GREAT-GRANDPARENTS | 7X GREAT-GRANDPARENTS | 8X GREAT-GRANDPARENTS | 9X GREAT-GRANDPARENTS |

THIS CHART STARTS WITH THE PARENTS OF 161.

9th GENERATION	10th GENERATION	11th GENERATION	12th GENERATION
THEIR FATHER	NAME	NAME	NAME
NAME	BORN	BORN	LIVED
BORN	DIED	DIED	NAME
DIED	MARRIED	MARRIED	LIVED
MARRIED	NOTES	NAME	NAME
NOTES		BORN	LIVED
		DIED	NAME
		NOTES	LIVED
	NAME	NAME	NAME
	BORN	BORN	LIVED
	DIED	DIED	NAME
	NOTES	MARRIED	LIVED
		NAME	NAME
		BORN	LIVED
		DIED	NAME
		NOTES	LIVED
THEIR MOTHER	NAME	NAME	NAME
NAME	BORN	BORN	LIVED
BORN	DIED	DIED	NAME
DIED	MARRIED	MARRIED	LIVED
NOTES	NOTES	NAME	NAME
		BORN	LIVED
		DIED	NAME
		NOTES	LIVED
	NAME	NAME	NAME
	BORN	BORN	LIVED
	DIED	DIED	NAME
	NOTES	MARRIED	LIVED
		NAME	NAME
		BORN	LIVED
		DIED	NAME
		NOTES	LIVED

| 6X GREAT-GRANDPARENTS | 7X GREAT-GRANDPARENTS | 8X GREAT-GRANDPARENTS | 9X GREAT-GRANDPARENTS |

THIS CHART STARTS WITH THE PARENTS OF 162.

9th GENERATION	10th GENERATION	11th GENERATION	12th GENERATION
THEIR FATHER	NAME	NAME	NAME
NAME	BORN	BORN	LIVED
BORN	DIED	DIED	NAME
DIED	MARRIED	MARRIED	LIVED
MARRIED	NOTES	NAME	NAME
NOTES		BORN	LIVED
		DIED	NAME
		NOTES	LIVED
	NAME	NAME	NAME
	BORN	BORN	LIVED
	DIED	DIED	NAME
	NOTES	MARRIED	LIVED
		NAME	NAME
		BORN	LIVED
		DIED	NAME
		NOTES	LIVED
THEIR MOTHER	NAME	NAME	NAME
NAME	BORN	BORN	LIVED
BORN	DIED	DIED	NAME
DIED	MARRIED	MARRIED	LIVED
NOTES	NOTES	NAME	NAME
		BORN	LIVED
		DIED	NAME
		NOTES	LIVED
	NAME	NAME	NAME
	BORN	BORN	LIVED
	DIED	DIED	NAME
	NOTES	MARRIED	LIVED
		NAME	NAME
		BORN	LIVED
		DIED	NAME
		NOTES	LIVED

| 6X GREAT-GRANDPARENTS | 7X GREAT-GRANDPARENTS | 8X GREAT-GRANDPARENTS | 9X GREAT-GRANDPARENTS |

THIS CHART STARTS WITH THE PARENTS OF 163.

9th GENERATION	10th GENERATION	11th GENERATION	12th GENERATION
THEIR FATHER NAME BORN DIED MARRIED NOTES	NAME BORN DIED MARRIED NOTES	NAME BORN DIED MARRIED	NAME LIVED
			NAME LIVED
		NAME BORN DIED NOTES	NAME LIVED
			NAME LIVED
			NAME LIVED
			NAME LIVED
	NAME BORN DIED NOTES	NAME BORN DIED MARRIED	NAME LIVED
			NAME LIVED
		NAME BORN DIED NOTES	NAME LIVED
			NAME LIVED
			NAME LIVED
			NAME LIVED
THEIR MOTHER NAME BORN DIED NOTES	NAME BORN DIED MARRIED NOTES	NAME BORN DIED MARRIED	NAME LIVED
			NAME LIVED
		NAME BORN DIED NOTES	NAME LIVED
			NAME LIVED
			NAME LIVED
			NAME LIVED
	NAME BORN DIED NOTES	NAME BORN DIED MARRIED	NAME LIVED
			NAME LIVED
		NAME BORN DIED NOTES	NAME LIVED
			NAME LIVED
			NAME LIVED
			NAME LIVED

| 6X GREAT-GRANDPARENTS | 7X GREAT-GRANDPARENTS | 8X GREAT-GRANDPARENTS | 9X GREAT-GRANDPARENTS |

THIS CHART STARTS WITH THE PARENTS OF 164.

9th GENERATION	10th GENERATION	11th GENERATION	12th GENERATION
THEIR FATHER	NAME	NAME	NAME
NAME	BORN	BORN	LIVED
BORN	DIED	DIED	NAME
DIED	MARRIED	MARRIED	LIVED
MARRIED	NOTES	NAME	NAME
NOTES		BORN	LIVED
		DIED	NAME
		NOTES	LIVED
	NAME	NAME	NAME
	BORN	BORN	LIVED
	DIED	DIED	NAME
	NOTES	MARRIED	LIVED
		NAME	NAME
		BORN	LIVED
		DIED	NAME
		NOTES	LIVED
THEIR MOTHER	NAME	NAME	NAME
NAME	BORN	BORN	LIVED
BORN	DIED	DIED	NAME
DIED	MARRIED	MARRIED	LIVED
NOTES	NOTES	NAME	NAME
		BORN	LIVED
		DIED	NAME
		NOTES	LIVED
	NAME	NAME	NAME
	BORN	BORN	LIVED
	DIED	DIED	NAME
	NOTES	MARRIED	LIVED
		NAME	NAME
		BORN	LIVED
		DIED	NAME
		NOTES	LIVED

| 6X GREAT-GRANDPARENTS | 7X GREAT-GRANDPARENTS | 8X GREAT-GRANDPARENTS | 9X GREAT-GRANDPARENTS |

THIS CHART STARTS WITH THE PARENTS OF 165.

9th GENERATION	10th GENERATION	11th GENERATION	12th GENERATION
THEIR FATHER	NAME	NAME	NAME
NAME	BORN	BORN	LIVED
BORN	DIED	DIED	NAME
DIED	MARRIED	MARRIED	LIVED
MARRIED	NOTES	NAME	NAME
NOTES		BORN	LIVED
		DIED	NAME
		NOTES	LIVED
	NAME	NAME	NAME
	BORN	BORN	LIVED
	DIED	DIED	NAME
	NOTES	MARRIED	LIVED
		NAME	NAME
		BORN	LIVED
		DIED	NAME
		NOTES	LIVED
THEIR MOTHER	NAME	NAME	NAME
NAME	BORN	BORN	LIVED
BORN	DIED	DIED	NAME
DIED	MARRIED	MARRIED	LIVED
NOTES	NOTES	NAME	NAME
		BORN	LIVED
		DIED	NAME
		NOTES	LIVED
	NAME	NAME	NAME
	BORN	BORN	LIVED
	DIED	DIED	NAME
	NOTES	MARRIED	LIVED
		NAME	NAME
		BORN	LIVED
		DIED	NAME
		NOTES	LIVED

6X GREAT-GRANDPARENTS	7X GREAT-GRANDPARENTS	8X GREAT-GRANDPARENTS	9X GREAT-GRANDPARENTS

THIS CHART STARTS WITH THE PARENTS OF 166.

9th GENERATION	10th GENERATION	11th GENERATION	12th GENERATION
THEIR FATHER	NAME	NAME	NAME
NAME	BORN	BORN	LIVED
BORN	DIED	DIED	NAME
DIED	MARRIED	MARRIED	LIVED
MARRIED	NOTES	NAME	NAME
NOTES		BORN	LIVED
		DIED	NAME
		NOTES	LIVED
	NAME	NAME	NAME
	BORN	BORN	LIVED
	DIED	DIED	NAME
	NOTES	MARRIED	LIVED
		NAME	NAME
		BORN	LIVED
		DIED	NAME
		NOTES	LIVED
THEIR MOTHER	NAME	NAME	NAME
NAME	BORN	BORN	LIVED
BORN	DIED	DIED	NAME
DIED	MARRIED	MARRIED	LIVED
NOTES	NOTES	NAME	NAME
		BORN	LIVED
		DIED	NAME
		NOTES	LIVED
	NAME	NAME	NAME
	BORN	BORN	LIVED
	DIED	DIED	NAME
	NOTES	MARRIED	LIVED
		NAME	NAME
		BORN	LIVED
		DIED	NAME
		NOTES	LIVED

| 6X GREAT-GRANDPARENTS | 7X GREAT-GRANDPARENTS | 8X GREAT-GRANDPARENTS | 9X GREAT-GRANDPARENTS |

THIS CHART STARTS WITH THE PARENTS OF 167.

9th GENERATION	10th GENERATION	11th GENERATION	12th GENERATION
THEIR FATHER NAME BORN DIED MARRIED NOTES	NAME BORN DIED MARRIED NOTES	NAME BORN DIED MARRIED	NAME LIVED
			NAME LIVED
		NAME BORN DIED NOTES	NAME LIVED
			NAME LIVED
			NAME LIVED
	NAME BORN DIED NOTES	NAME BORN DIED MARRIED	NAME LIVED
			NAME LIVED
		NAME BORN DIED NOTES	NAME LIVED
			NAME LIVED
			NAME LIVED
THEIR MOTHER NAME BORN DIED NOTES	NAME BORN DIED MARRIED NOTES	NAME BORN DIED MARRIED	NAME LIVED
			NAME LIVED
		NAME BORN DIED NOTES	NAME LIVED
			NAME LIVED
			NAME LIVED
	NAME BORN DIED NOTES	NAME BORN DIED MARRIED	NAME LIVED
			NAME LIVED
		NAME BORN DIED NOTES	NAME LIVED
			NAME LIVED

| 6X GREAT-GRANDPARENTS | 7X GREAT-GRANDPARENTS | 8X GREAT-GRANDPARENTS | 9X GREAT-GRANDPARENTS |

THIS CHART STARTS WITH THE PARENTS OF 168.

9th GENERATION	10th GENERATION	11th GENERATION	12th GENERATION
THEIR FATHER	NAME	NAME	NAME
NAME	BORN	BORN	LIVED
BORN	DIED	DIED	NAME
DIED	MARRIED	MARRIED	LIVED
MARRIED	NOTES	NAME	NAME
NOTES		BORN	LIVED
		DIED	NAME
		NOTES	LIVED
	NAME	NAME	NAME
	BORN	BORN	LIVED
	DIED	DIED	NAME
	NOTES	MARRIED	LIVED
		NAME	NAME
		BORN	LIVED
		DIED	NAME
		NOTES	LIVED
THEIR MOTHER	NAME	NAME	NAME
NAME	BORN	BORN	LIVED
BORN	DIED	DIED	NAME
DIED	MARRIED	MARRIED	LIVED
NOTES	NOTES	NAME	NAME
		BORN	LIVED
		DIED	NAME
		NOTES	LIVED
	NAME	NAME	NAME
	BORN	BORN	LIVED
	DIED	DIED	NAME
	NOTES	MARRIED	LIVED
		NAME	NAME
		BORN	LIVED
		DIED	NAME
		NOTES	LIVED

| 6X GREAT-GRANDPARENTS | 7X GREAT-GRANDPARENTS | 8X GREAT-GRANDPARENTS | 9X GREAT-GRANDPARENTS |

THIS CHART STARTS WITH THE PARENTS OF 169.

9th GENERATION	10th GENERATION	11th GENERATION	12th GENERATION
THEIR FATHER	NAME	NAME	NAME
NAME	BORN	BORN	LIVED
BORN	DIED	DIED	NAME
DIED	MARRIED	MARRIED	LIVED
MARRIED	NOTES	NAME	NAME
NOTES		BORN	LIVED
		DIED	NAME
		NOTES	LIVED
	NAME	NAME	NAME
	BORN	BORN	LIVED
	DIED	DIED	NAME
	NOTES	MARRIED	LIVED
		NAME	NAME
		BORN	LIVED
		DIED	NAME
		NOTES	LIVED
THEIR MOTHER	NAME	NAME	NAME
NAME	BORN	BORN	LIVED
BORN	DIED	DIED	NAME
DIED	MARRIED	MARRIED	LIVED
NOTES	NOTES	NAME	NAME
		BORN	LIVED
		DIED	NAME
		NOTES	LIVED
	NAME	NAME	NAME
	BORN	BORN	LIVED
	DIED	DIED	NAME
	NOTES	MARRIED	LIVED
		NAME	NAME
		BORN	LIVED
		DIED	NAME
		NOTES	LIVED

| 6X GREAT-GRANDPARENTS | 7X GREAT-GRANDPARENTS | 8X GREAT-GRANDPARENTS | 9X GREAT-GRANDPARENTS |

9th GENERATION	10th GENERATION	11th GENERATION	12th GENERATION
THEIR FATHER	NAME	NAME	NAME
NAME	BORN	BORN	LIVED
BORN	DIED	DIED	NAME
DIED	MARRIED	MARRIED	LIVED
MARRIED	NOTES	NAME	NAME
NOTES		BORN	LIVED
		DIED	NAME
		NOTES	LIVED
	NAME	NAME	NAME
	BORN	BORN	LIVED
	DIED	DIED	NAME
	NOTES	MARRIED	LIVED
		NAME	NAME
		BORN	LIVED
		DIED	NAME
		NOTES	LIVED
THEIR MOTHER	NAME	NAME	NAME
NAME	BORN	BORN	LIVED
BORN	DIED	DIED	NAME
DIED	MARRIED	MARRIED	LIVED
NOTES	NOTES	NAME	NAME
		BORN	LIVED
		DIED	NAME
		NOTES	LIVED
	NAME	NAME	NAME
	BORN	BORN	LIVED
	DIED	DIED	NAME
	NOTES	MARRIED	LIVED
		NAME	NAME
		BORN	LIVED
		DIED	NAME
		NOTES	LIVED

| 6X GREAT-GRANDPARENTS | 7X GREAT-GRANDPARENTS | 8X GREAT-GRANDPARENTS | 9X GREAT-GRANDPARENTS |

THIS CHART STARTS WITH THE PARENTS OF 171.

9th GENERATION	10th GENERATION	11th GENERATION	12th GENERATION
THEIR FATHER	NAME	NAME	NAME
NAME	BORN	BORN	LIVED
BORN	DIED	DIED	NAME
DIED	MARRIED	MARRIED	LIVED
MARRIED	NOTES	NAME	NAME
NOTES		BORN	LIVED
		DIED	NAME
		NOTES	LIVED
	NAME	NAME	NAME
	BORN	BORN	LIVED
	DIED	DIED	NAME
	NOTES	MARRIED	LIVED
		NAME	NAME
		BORN	LIVED
		DIED	NAME
		NOTES	LIVED
THEIR MOTHER	NAME	NAME	NAME
NAME	BORN	BORN	LIVED
BORN	DIED	DIED	NAME
DIED	MARRIED	MARRIED	LIVED
NOTES	NOTES	NAME	NAME
		BORN	LIVED
		DIED	NAME
		NOTES	LIVED
	NAME	NAME	NAME
	BORN	BORN	LIVED
	DIED	DIED	NAME
	NOTES	MARRIED	LIVED
		NAME	NAME
		BORN	LIVED
		DIED	NAME
		NOTES	LIVED

6X GREAT-GRANDPARENTS	7X GREAT-GRANDPARENTS	8X GREAT-GRANDPARENTS	9X GREAT-GRANDPARENTS

THIS CHART STARTS WITH THE PARENTS OF 172.

9th GENERATION	10th GENERATION	11th GENERATION	12th GENERATION
THEIR FATHER	NAME	NAME	NAME
NAME	BORN	BORN	LIVED
BORN	DIED	DIED	NAME
DIED	MARRIED	MARRIED	LIVED
MARRIED	NOTES	NAME	NAME
NOTES		BORN	LIVED
		DIED	NAME
		NOTES	LIVED
	NAME	NAME	NAME
	BORN	BORN	LIVED
	DIED	DIED	NAME
	NOTES	MARRIED	LIVED
		NAME	NAME
		BORN	LIVED
		DIED	NAME
		NOTES	LIVED
THEIR MOTHER	NAME	NAME	NAME
NAME	BORN	BORN	LIVED
BORN	DIED	DIED	NAME
DIED	MARRIED	MARRIED	LIVED
NOTES	NOTES	NAME	NAME
		BORN	LIVED
		DIED	NAME
		NOTES	LIVED
	NAME	NAME	NAME
	BORN	BORN	LIVED
	DIED	DIED	NAME
	NOTES	MARRIED	LIVED
		NAME	NAME
		BORN	LIVED
		DIED	NAME
		NOTES	LIVED

| 6X GREAT-GRANDPARENTS | 7X GREAT-GRANDPARENTS | 8X GREAT-GRANDPARENTS | 9X GREAT-GRANDPARENTS |

9th GENERATION	10th GENERATION	11th GENERATION	12th GENERATION
THEIR FATHER	NAME	NAME	NAME
NAME	BORN	BORN	LIVED
BORN	DIED	DIED	NAME
DIED	MARRIED	MARRIED	LIVED
MARRIED	NOTES	NAME	NAME
NOTES		BORN	LIVED
		DIED	NAME
		NOTES	LIVED
	NAME	NAME	NAME
	BORN	BORN	LIVED
	DIED	DIED	NAME
	NOTES	MARRIED	LIVED
		NAME	NAME
		BORN	LIVED
		DIED	NAME
		NOTES	LIVED
THEIR MOTHER	NAME	NAME	NAME
NAME	BORN	BORN	LIVED
BORN	DIED	DIED	NAME
DIED	MARRIED	MARRIED	LIVED
NOTES	NOTES	NAME	NAME
		BORN	LIVED
		DIED	NAME
		NOTES	LIVED
	NAME	NAME	NAME
	BORN	BORN	LIVED
	DIED	DIED	NAME
	NOTES	MARRIED	LIVED
		NAME	NAME
		BORN	LIVED
		DIED	NAME
		NOTES	LIVED

6X GREAT-GRANDPARENTS	7X GREAT-GRANDPARENTS	8X GREAT-GRANDPARENTS	9X GREAT-GRANDPARENTS

THIS CHART STARTS WITH THE PARENTS OF 174.

9th GENERATION	10th GENERATION	11th GENERATION	12th GENERATION
THEIR FATHER	NAME	NAME	NAME
NAME	BORN	BORN	LIVED
BORN	DIED	DIED	NAME
DIED	MARRIED	MARRIED	LIVED
MARRIED	NOTES	NAME	NAME
NOTES		BORN	LIVED
		DIED	NAME
		NOTES	LIVED
	NAME	NAME	NAME
	BORN	BORN	LIVED
	DIED	DIED	NAME
	NOTES	MARRIED	LIVED
		NAME	NAME
		BORN	LIVED
		DIED	NAME
		NOTES	LIVED
THEIR MOTHER	NAME	NAME	NAME
NAME	BORN	BORN	LIVED
BORN	DIED	DIED	NAME
DIED	MARRIED	MARRIED	LIVED
NOTES	NOTES	NAME	NAME
		BORN	LIVED
		DIED	NAME
		NOTES	LIVED
	NAME	NAME	NAME
	BORN	BORN	LIVED
	DIED	DIED	NAME
	NOTES	MARRIED	LIVED
		NAME	NAME
		BORN	LIVED
		DIED	NAME
		NOTES	LIVED

6X GREAT-GRANDPARENTS	7X GREAT-GRANDPARENTS	8X GREAT-GRANDPARENTS	9X GREAT-GRANDPARENTS

THIS CHART STARTS WITH THE PARENTS OF 175.

9th GENERATION	10th GENERATION	11th GENERATION	12th GENERATION
THEIR FATHER	NAME	NAME	NAME
NAME	BORN	BORN	LIVED
BORN	DIED	DIED	NAME
DIED	MARRIED	MARRIED	LIVED
MARRIED	NOTES	NAME	NAME
NOTES		BORN	LIVED
		DIED	NAME
		NOTES	LIVED
	NAME	NAME	NAME
	BORN	BORN	LIVED
	DIED	DIED	NAME
	NOTES	MARRIED	LIVED
		NAME	NAME
		BORN	LIVED
		DIED	NAME
		NOTES	LIVED
THEIR MOTHER	NAME	NAME	NAME
NAME	BORN	BORN	LIVED
BORN	DIED	DIED	NAME
DIED	MARRIED	MARRIED	LIVED
NOTES	NOTES	NAME	NAME
		BORN	LIVED
		DIED	NAME
		NOTES	LIVED
	NAME	NAME	NAME
	BORN	BORN	LIVED
	DIED	DIED	NAME
	NOTES	MARRIED	LIVED
		NAME	NAME
		BORN	LIVED
		DIED	NAME
		NOTES	LIVED

6X GREAT-GRANDPARENTS	7X GREAT-GRANDPARENTS	8X GREAT-GRANDPARENTS	9X GREAT-GRANDPARENTS

THIS CHART STARTS WITH THE PARENTS OF 176.

9th GENERATION	10th GENERATION	11th GENERATION	12th GENERATION
THEIR FATHER	NAME	NAME	NAME
NAME	BORN	BORN	LIVED
BORN	DIED	DIED	NAME
DIED	MARRIED	MARRIED	LIVED
MARRIED	NOTES	NAME	NAME
NOTES		BORN	LIVED
		DIED	NAME
		NOTES	LIVED
	NAME	NAME	NAME
	BORN	BORN	LIVED
	DIED	DIED	NAME
	NOTES	MARRIED	LIVED
		NAME	NAME
		BORN	LIVED
		DIED	NAME
		NOTES	LIVED
THEIR MOTHER	NAME	NAME	NAME
NAME	BORN	BORN	LIVED
BORN	DIED	DIED	NAME
DIED	MARRIED	MARRIED	LIVED
NOTES	NOTES	NAME	NAME
		BORN	LIVED
		DIED	NAME
		NOTES	LIVED
	NAME	NAME	NAME
	BORN	BORN	LIVED
	DIED	DIED	NAME
	NOTES	MARRIED	LIVED
		NAME	NAME
		BORN	LIVED
		DIED	NAME
		NOTES	LIVED

6X GREAT-GRANDPARENTS	7X GREAT-GRANDPARENTS	8X GREAT-GRANDPARENTS	9X GREAT-GRANDPARENTS

THIS CHART STARTS WITH THE PARENTS OF 177

9th GENERATION	10th GENERATION	11th GENERATION	12th GENERATION
THEIR FATHER	NAME	NAME	NAME
NAME	BORN	BORN	LIVED
BORN	DIED	DIED	NAME
DIED	MARRIED	MARRIED	LIVED
MARRIED	NOTES	NAME	NAME
NOTES		BORN	LIVED
		DIED	NAME
		NOTES	LIVED
	NAME	NAME	NAME
	BORN	BORN	LIVED
	DIED	DIED	NAME
	NOTES	MARRIED	LIVED
		NAME	NAME
		BORN	LIVED
		DIED	NAME
		NOTES	LIVED
THEIR MOTHER	NAME	NAME	NAME
NAME	BORN	BORN	LIVED
BORN	DIED	DIED	NAME
DIED	MARRIED	MARRIED	LIVED
NOTES	NOTES	NAME	NAME
		BORN	LIVED
		DIED	NAME
		NOTES	LIVED
	NAME	NAME	NAME
	BORN	BORN	LIVED
	DIED	DIED	NAME
	NOTES	MARRIED	LIVED
		NAME	NAME
		BORN	LIVED
		DIED	NAME
		NOTES	LIVED

| 6X GREAT-GRANDPARENTS | 7X GREAT-GRANDPARENTS | 8X GREAT-GRANDPARENTS | 9X GREAT-GRANDPARENTS |

THIS CHART STARTS WITH THE PARENTS OF 178.

9th GENERATION	10th GENERATION	11th GENERATION	12th GENERATION
THEIR FATHER NAME BORN DIED MARRIED NOTES	NAME BORN DIED MARRIED NOTES	NAME BORN DIED MARRIED	NAME LIVED NAME LIVED
		NAME BORN DIED NOTES	NAME LIVED NAME LIVED
	NAME BORN DIED NOTES	NAME BORN DIED MARRIED	NAME LIVED NAME LIVED
		NAME BORN DIED NOTES	NAME LIVED NAME LIVED
THEIR MOTHER NAME BORN DIED NOTES	NAME BORN DIED MARRIED NOTES	NAME BORN DIED MARRIED	NAME LIVED NAME LIVED
		NAME BORN DIED NOTES	NAME LIVED NAME LIVED
	NAME BORN DIED NOTES	NAME BORN DIED MARRIED	NAME LIVED NAME LIVED
		NAME BORN DIED NOTES	NAME LIVED NAME LIVED

6X GREAT-GRANDPARENTS	7X GREAT-GRANDPARENTS	8X GREAT-GRANDPARENTS	9X GREAT-GRANDPARENTS

9th GENERATION	10th GENERATION	11th GENERATION	12th GENERATION
THEIR FATHER	NAME	NAME	NAME
NAME	BORN	BORN	LIVED
BORN	DIED	DIED	NAME
DIED	MARRIED	MARRIED	LIVED
MARRIED	NOTES	NAME	NAME
NOTES		BORN	LIVED
		DIED	NAME
		NOTES	LIVED
	NAME	NAME	NAME
	BORN	BORN	LIVED
	DIED	DIED	NAME
	NOTES	MARRIED	LIVED
		NAME	NAME
		BORN	LIVED
		DIED	NAME
		NOTES	LIVED
THEIR MOTHER	NAME	NAME	NAME
NAME	BORN	BORN	LIVED
BORN	DIED	DIED	NAME
DIED	MARRIED	MARRIED	LIVED
NOTES	NOTES	NAME	NAME
		BORN	LIVED
		DIED	NAME
		NOTES	LIVED
	NAME	NAME	NAME
	BORN	BORN	LIVED
	DIED	DIED	NAME
	NOTES	MARRIED	LIVED
		NAME	NAME
		BORN	LIVED
		DIED	NAME
		NOTES	LIVED

6X GREAT-GRANDPARENTS	7X GREAT-GRANDPARENTS	8X GREAT-GRANDPARENTS	9X GREAT-GRANDPARENTS

THIS CHART STARTS WITH THE PARENTS OF 180.

9th GENERATION	10th GENERATION	11th GENERATION	12th GENERATION
THEIR FATHER	NAME	NAME	NAME
NAME	BORN	BORN	LIVED
BORN	DIED	DIED	NAME
DIED	MARRIED	MARRIED	LIVED
MARRIED	NOTES	NAME	NAME
NOTES		BORN	LIVED
		DIED	NAME
		NOTES	LIVED
	NAME	NAME	NAME
	BORN	BORN	LIVED
	DIED	DIED	NAME
	NOTES	MARRIED	LIVED
		NAME	NAME
		BORN	LIVED
		DIED	NAME
		NOTES	LIVED
THEIR MOTHER	NAME	NAME	NAME
NAME	BORN	BORN	LIVED
BORN	DIED	DIED	NAME
DIED	MARRIED	MARRIED	LIVED
NOTES	NOTES	NAME	NAME
		BORN	LIVED
		DIED	NAME
		NOTES	LIVED
	NAME	NAME	NAME
	BORN	BORN	LIVED
	DIED	DIED	NAME
	NOTES	MARRIED	LIVED
		NAME	NAME
		BORN	LIVED
		DIED	NAME
		NOTES	LIVED

| 6X GREAT-GRANDPARENTS | 7X GREAT-GRANDPARENTS | 8X GREAT-GRANDPARENTS | 9X GREAT-GRANDPARENTS |

9th GENERATION	10th GENERATION	11th GENERATION	12th GENERATION
THEIR FATHER	NAME	NAME	NAME
NAME	BORN	BORN	LIVED
BORN	DIED	DIED	NAME
DIED	MARRIED	MARRIED	LIVED
MARRIED	NOTES	NAME	NAME
NOTES		BORN	LIVED
		DIED	NAME
		NOTES	LIVED
	NAME	NAME	NAME
	BORN	BORN	LIVED
	DIED	DIED	NAME
	NOTES	MARRIED	LIVED
		NAME	NAME
		BORN	LIVED
		DIED	NAME
		NOTES	LIVED
THEIR MOTHER	NAME	NAME	NAME
NAME	BORN	BORN	LIVED
BORN	DIED	DIED	NAME
DIED	MARRIED	MARRIED	LIVED
NOTES	NOTES	NAME	NAME
		BORN	LIVED
		DIED	NAME
		NOTES	LIVED
	NAME	NAME	NAME
	BORN	BORN	LIVED
	DIED	DIED	NAME
	NOTES	MARRIED	LIVED
		NAME	NAME
		BORN	LIVED
		DIED	NAME
		NOTES	LIVED

| 6X GREAT-GRANDPARENTS | 7X GREAT-GRANDPARENTS | 8X GREAT-GRANDPARENTS | 9X GREAT-GRANDPARENTS |

THIS CHART STARTS WITH THE PARENTS OF 182.

9th GENERATION	10th GENERATION	11th GENERATION	12th GENERATION
THEIR FATHER NAME BORN DIED MARRIED NOTES	NAME BORN DIED MARRIED NOTES	NAME BORN DIED MARRIED	NAME LIVED
			NAME LIVED
		NAME BORN DIED NOTES	NAME LIVED
			NAME LIVED
	NAME BORN DIED NOTES	NAME BORN DIED MARRIED	NAME LIVED
			NAME LIVED
		NAME BORN DIED NOTES	NAME LIVED
			NAME LIVED
THEIR MOTHER NAME BORN DIED NOTES	NAME BORN DIED MARRIED NOTES	NAME BORN DIED MARRIED	NAME LIVED
			NAME LIVED
		NAME BORN DIED NOTES	NAME LIVED
			NAME LIVED
	NAME BORN DIED NOTES	NAME BORN DIED MARRIED	NAME LIVED
			NAME LIVED
		NAME BORN DIED NOTES	NAME LIVED
			NAME LIVED

| 6X GREAT-GRANDPARENTS | 7X GREAT-GRANDPARENTS | 8X GREAT-GRANDPARENTS | 9X GREAT-GRANDPARENTS |

THIS CHART STARTS WITH THE PARENTS OF 183.

9th GENERATION	10th GENERATION	11th GENERATION	12th GENERATION
THEIR FATHER	NAME	NAME	NAME
NAME	BORN	BORN	LIVED
BORN	DIED	DIED	NAME
DIED	MARRIED	MARRIED	LIVED
MARRIED	NOTES	NAME	NAME
NOTES		BORN	LIVED
		DIED	NAME
		NOTES	LIVED
	NAME	NAME	NAME
	BORN	BORN	LIVED
	DIED	DIED	NAME
	NOTES	MARRIED	LIVED
		NAME	NAME
		BORN	LIVED
		DIED	NAME
		NOTES	LIVED
THEIR MOTHER	NAME	NAME	NAME
NAME	BORN	BORN	LIVED
BORN	DIED	DIED	NAME
DIED	MARRIED	MARRIED	LIVED
NOTES	NOTES	NAME	NAME
		BORN	LIVED
		DIED	NAME
		NOTES	LIVED
	NAME	NAME	NAME
	BORN	BORN	LIVED
	DIED	DIED	NAME
	NOTES	MARRIED	LIVED
		NAME	NAME
		BORN	LIVED
		DIED	NAME
		NOTES	LIVED

| 6X GREAT-GRANDPARENTS | 7X GREAT-GRANDPARENTS | 8X GREAT-GRANDPARENTS | 9X GREAT-GRANDPARENTS |

THIS CHART STARTS WITH THE PARENTS OF 184.

9th GENERATION	10th GENERATION	11th GENERATION	12th GENERATION
THEIR FATHER	NAME	NAME	NAME
NAME	BORN	BORN	LIVED
BORN	DIED	DIED	NAME
DIED	MARRIED	MARRIED	LIVED
MARRIED	NOTES	NAME	NAME
NOTES		BORN	LIVED
		DIED	NAME
		NOTES	LIVED
	NAME	NAME	NAME
	BORN	BORN	LIVED
	DIED	DIED	NAME
	NOTES	MARRIED	LIVED
		NAME	NAME
		BORN	LIVED
		DIED	NAME
		NOTES	LIVED
THEIR MOTHER	NAME	NAME	NAME
NAME	BORN	BORN	LIVED
BORN	DIED	DIED	NAME
DIED	MARRIED	MARRIED	LIVED
NOTES	NOTES	NAME	NAME
		BORN	LIVED
		DIED	NAME
		NOTES	LIVED
	NAME	NAME	NAME
	BORN	BORN	LIVED
	DIED	DIED	NAME
	NOTES	MARRIED	LIVED
		NAME	NAME
		BORN	LIVED
		DIED	NAME
		NOTES	LIVED

| 6X GREAT-GRANDPARENTS | 7X GREAT-GRANDPARENTS | 8X GREAT-GRANDPARENTS | 9X GREAT-GRANDPARENTS |

THIS CHART STARTS WITH THE PARENTS OF 185.

9th GENERATION	10th GENERATION	11th GENERATION	12th GENERATION
THEIR FATHER	NAME	NAME	NAME
NAME	BORN	BORN	LIVED
BORN	DIED	DIED	NAME
DIED	MARRIED	MARRIED	LIVED
MARRIED	NOTES	NAME	NAME
NOTES		BORN	LIVED
		DIED	NAME
		NOTES	LIVED
	NAME	NAME	NAME
	BORN	BORN	LIVED
	DIED	DIED	NAME
	NOTES	MARRIED	LIVED
		NAME	NAME
		BORN	LIVED
		DIED	NAME
		NOTES	LIVED
THEIR MOTHER	NAME	NAME	NAME
NAME	BORN	BORN	LIVED
BORN	DIED	DIED	NAME
DIED	MARRIED	MARRIED	LIVED
NOTES	NOTES	NAME	NAME
		BORN	LIVED
		DIED	NAME
		NOTES	LIVED
	NAME	NAME	NAME
	BORN	BORN	LIVED
	DIED	DIED	NAME
	NOTES	MARRIED	LIVED
		NAME	NAME
		BORN	LIVED
		DIED	NAME
		NOTES	LIVED

| 6X GREAT-GRANDPARENTS | 7X GREAT-GRANDPARENTS | 8X GREAT-GRANDPARENTS | 9X GREAT-GRANDPARENTS |

THIS CHART STARTS WITH THE PARENTS OF 186.

9th GENERATION	10th GENERATION	11th GENERATION	12th GENERATION
THEIR FATHER	NAME	NAME	NAME
NAME	BORN	BORN	LIVED
BORN	DIED	DIED	NAME
DIED	MARRIED	MARRIED	LIVED
MARRIED	NOTES	NAME	NAME
NOTES		BORN	LIVED
		DIED	NAME
		NOTES	LIVED
	NAME	NAME	NAME
	BORN	BORN	LIVED
	DIED	DIED	NAME
	NOTES	MARRIED	LIVED
		NAME	NAME
		BORN	LIVED
		DIED	NAME
		NOTES	LIVED
THEIR MOTHER	NAME	NAME	NAME
NAME	BORN	BORN	LIVED
BORN	DIED	DIED	NAME
DIED	MARRIED	MARRIED	LIVED
NOTES	NOTES	NAME	NAME
		BORN	LIVED
		DIED	NAME
		NOTES	LIVED
	NAME	NAME	NAME
	BORN	BORN	LIVED
	DIED	DIED	NAME
	NOTES	MARRIED	LIVED
		NAME	NAME
		BORN	LIVED
		DIED	NAME
		NOTES	LIVED

6X GREAT-GRANDPARENTS	7X GREAT-GRANDPARENTS	8X GREAT-GRANDPARENTS	9X GREAT-GRANDPARENTS

THIS CHART STARTS WITH THE PARENTS OF 187

9th GENERATION	10th GENERATION	11th GENERATION	12th GENERATION
THEIR FATHER	NAME	NAME	NAME
NAME	BORN	BORN	LIVED
BORN	DIED	DIED	NAME
DIED	MARRIED	MARRIED	LIVED
MARRIED	NOTES	NAME	NAME
NOTES		BORN	LIVED
		DIED	NAME
		NOTES	LIVED
	NAME	NAME	NAME
	BORN	BORN	LIVED
	DIED	DIED	NAME
	NOTES	MARRIED	LIVED
		NAME	NAME
		BORN	LIVED
		DIED	NAME
		NOTES	LIVED
THEIR MOTHER	NAME	NAME	NAME
NAME	BORN	BORN	LIVED
BORN	DIED	DIED	NAME
DIED	MARRIED	MARRIED	LIVED
NOTES	NOTES	NAME	NAME
		BORN	LIVED
		DIED	NAME
		NOTES	LIVED
	NAME	NAME	NAME
	BORN	BORN	LIVED
	DIED	DIED	NAME
	NOTES	MARRIED	LIVED
		NAME	NAME
		BORN	LIVED
		DIED	NAME
		NOTES	LIVED

6X GREAT-GRANDPARENTS	7X GREAT-GRANDPARENTS	8X GREAT-GRANDPARENTS	9X GREAT-GRANDPARENTS

THIS CHART STARTS WITH THE PARENTS OF 188.

9th GENERATION	10th GENERATION	11th GENERATION	12th GENERATION
THEIR FATHER	NAME	NAME	NAME
NAME	BORN	BORN	LIVED
BORN	DIED	DIED	NAME
DIED	MARRIED	MARRIED	LIVED
MARRIED	NOTES	NAME	NAME
NOTES		BORN	LIVED
		DIED	NAME
		NOTES	LIVED
	NAME	NAME	NAME
	BORN	BORN	LIVED
	DIED	DIED	NAME
	NOTES	MARRIED	LIVED
		NAME	NAME
		BORN	LIVED
		DIED	NAME
		NOTES	LIVED
THEIR MOTHER	NAME	NAME	NAME
NAME	BORN	BORN	LIVED
BORN	DIED	DIED	NAME
DIED	MARRIED	MARRIED	LIVED
NOTES	NOTES	NAME	NAME
		BORN	LIVED
		DIED	NAME
		NOTES	LIVED
	NAME	NAME	NAME
	BORN	BORN	LIVED
	DIED	DIED	NAME
	NOTES	MARRIED	LIVED
		NAME	NAME
		BORN	LIVED
		DIED	NAME
		NOTES	LIVED

6X GREAT-GRANDPARENTS	7X GREAT-GRANDPARENTS	8X GREAT-GRANDPARENTS	9X GREAT-GRANDPARENTS

9th GENERATION	10th GENERATION	11th GENERATION	12th GENERATION
THEIR FATHER	NAME	NAME	NAME
NAME	BORN	BORN	LIVED
BORN	DIED	DIED	NAME
DIED	MARRIED	MARRIED	LIVED
MARRIED	NOTES	NAME	NAME
NOTES		BORN	LIVED
		DIED	NAME
		NOTES	LIVED
	NAME	NAME	NAME
	BORN	BORN	LIVED
	DIED	DIED	NAME
	NOTES	MARRIED	LIVED
		NAME	NAME
		BORN	LIVED
		DIED	NAME
		NOTES	LIVED
THEIR MOTHER	NAME	NAME	NAME
NAME	BORN	BORN	LIVED
BORN	DIED	DIED	NAME
DIED	MARRIED	MARRIED	LIVED
NOTES	NOTES	NAME	NAME
		BORN	LIVED
		DIED	NAME
		NOTES	LIVED
	NAME	NAME	NAME
	BORN	BORN	LIVED
	DIED	DIED	NAME
	NOTES	MARRIED	LIVED
		NAME	NAME
		BORN	LIVED
		DIED	NAME
		NOTES	LIVED

6X GREAT-GRANDPARENTS	7X GREAT-GRANDPARENTS	8X GREAT-GRANDPARENTS	9X GREAT-GRANDPARENTS

THIS CHART STARTS WITH THE PARENTS OF 190.

9th GENERATION	10th GENERATION	11th GENERATION	12th GENERATION
THEIR FATHER NAME BORN DIED MARRIED NOTES	NAME BORN DIED MARRIED NOTES	NAME BORN DIED MARRIED	NAME LIVED
			NAME LIVED
		NAME BORN DIED NOTES	NAME LIVED
			NAME LIVED
			NAME LIVED
	NAME BORN DIED NOTES	NAME BORN DIED MARRIED	NAME LIVED
			NAME LIVED
		NAME BORN DIED NOTES	NAME LIVED
			NAME LIVED
THEIR MOTHER NAME BORN DIED NOTES	NAME BORN DIED MARRIED NOTES	NAME BORN DIED MARRIED	NAME LIVED
			NAME LIVED
		NAME BORN DIED NOTES	NAME LIVED
			NAME LIVED
	NAME BORN DIED NOTES	NAME BORN DIED MARRIED	NAME LIVED
			NAME LIVED
		NAME BORN DIED NOTES	NAME LIVED
			NAME LIVED

6X GREAT-GRANDPARENTS	7X GREAT-GRANDPARENTS	8X GREAT-GRANDPARENTS	9X GREAT-GRANDPARENTS

THIS CHART STARTS WITH THE PARENTS OF 191.

9th GENERATION	10th GENERATION	11th GENERATION	12th GENERATION
THEIR FATHER	NAME	NAME	NAME
NAME	BORN	BORN	LIVED
BORN	DIED	DIED	NAME
DIED	MARRIED	MARRIED	LIVED
MARRIED	NOTES	NAME	NAME
NOTES		BORN	LIVED
		DIED	NAME
		NOTES	LIVED
	NAME	NAME	NAME
	BORN	BORN	LIVED
	DIED	DIED	NAME
	NOTES	MARRIED	LIVED
		NAME	NAME
		BORN	LIVED
		DIED	NAME
		NOTES	LIVED
THEIR MOTHER	NAME	NAME	NAME
NAME	BORN	BORN	LIVED
BORN	DIED	DIED	NAME
DIED	MARRIED	MARRIED	LIVED
NOTES	NOTES	NAME	NAME
		BORN	LIVED
		DIED	NAME
		NOTES	LIVED
	NAME	NAME	NAME
	BORN	BORN	LIVED
	DIED	DIED	NAME
	NOTES	MARRIED	LIVED
		NAME	NAME
		BORN	LIVED
		DIED	NAME
		NOTES	LIVED

6X GREAT-GRANDPARENTS	7X GREAT-GRANDPARENTS	8X GREAT-GRANDPARENTS	9X GREAT-GRANDPARENTS

THIS CHART STARTS WITH THE PARENTS OF 192.

9th GENERATION	10th GENERATION	11th GENERATION	12th GENERATION
THEIR FATHER	NAME	NAME	NAME
NAME	BORN	BORN	LIVED
BORN	DIED	DIED	NAME
DIED	MARRIED	MARRIED	LIVED
MARRIED	NOTES	NAME	NAME
NOTES		BORN	LIVED
		DIED	NAME
		NOTES	LIVED
	NAME	NAME	NAME
	BORN	BORN	LIVED
	DIED	DIED	NAME
	NOTES	MARRIED	LIVED
		NAME	NAME
		BORN	LIVED
		DIED	NAME
		NOTES	LIVED
THEIR MOTHER	NAME	NAME	NAME
NAME	BORN	BORN	LIVED
BORN	DIED	DIED	NAME
DIED	MARRIED	MARRIED	LIVED
NOTES	NOTES	NAME	NAME
		BORN	LIVED
		DIED	NAME
		NOTES	LIVED
	NAME	NAME	NAME
	BORN	BORN	LIVED
	DIED	DIED	NAME
	NOTES	MARRIED	LIVED
		NAME	NAME
		BORN	LIVED
		DIED	NAME
		NOTES	LIVED

6X GREAT-GRANDPARENTS	7X GREAT-GRANDPARENTS	8X GREAT-GRANDPARENTS	9X GREAT-GRANDPARENTS

THIS CHART STARTS WITH THE PARENTS OF 193.

9th GENERATION	10th GENERATION	11th GENERATION	12th GENERATION
THEIR FATHER	NAME	NAME	NAME
NAME	BORN	BORN	LIVED
BORN	DIED	DIED	NAME
DIED	MARRIED	MARRIED	LIVED
MARRIED	NOTES	NAME	NAME
NOTES		BORN	LIVED
		DIED	NAME
		NOTES	LIVED
	NAME	NAME	NAME
	BORN	BORN	LIVED
	DIED	DIED	NAME
	NOTES	MARRIED	LIVED
		NAME	NAME
		BORN	LIVED
		DIED	NAME
		NOTES	LIVED
THEIR MOTHER	NAME	NAME	NAME
NAME	BORN	BORN	LIVED
BORN	DIED	DIED	NAME
DIED	MARRIED	MARRIED	LIVED
NOTES	NOTES	NAME	NAME
		BORN	LIVED
		DIED	NAME
		NOTES	LIVED
	NAME	NAME	NAME
	BORN	BORN	LIVED
	DIED	DIED	NAME
	NOTES	MARRIED	LIVED
		NAME	NAME
		BORN	LIVED
		DIED	NAME
		NOTES	LIVED
6X GREAT-GRANDPARENTS	7X GREAT-GRANDPARENTS	8X GREAT-GRANDPARENTS	9X GREAT-GRANDPARENTS

THIS CHART STARTS WITH THE PARENTS OF 194.

9th GENERATION	10th GENERATION	11th GENERATION	12th GENERATION
THEIR FATHER	NAME	NAME	NAME
NAME	BORN	BORN	LIVED
BORN	DIED	DIED	NAME
DIED	MARRIED	MARRIED	LIVED
MARRIED	NOTES	NAME	NAME
NOTES		BORN	LIVED
		DIED	NAME
		NOTES	LIVED
	NAME	NAME	NAME
	BORN	BORN	LIVED
	DIED	DIED	NAME
	NOTES	MARRIED	LIVED
		NAME	NAME
		BORN	LIVED
		DIED	NAME
		NOTES	LIVED
THEIR MOTHER	NAME	NAME	NAME
NAME	BORN	BORN	LIVED
BORN	DIED	DIED	NAME
DIED	MARRIED	MARRIED	LIVED
NOTES	NOTES	NAME	NAME
		BORN	LIVED
		DIED	NAME
		NOTES	LIVED
	NAME	NAME	NAME
	BORN	BORN	LIVED
	DIED	DIED	NAME
	NOTES	MARRIED	LIVED
		NAME	NAME
		BORN	LIVED
		DIED	NAME
		NOTES	LIVED

| 6X GREAT-GRANDPARENTS | 7X GREAT-GRANDPARENTS | 8X GREAT-GRANDPARENTS | 9X GREAT-GRANDPARENTS |

THIS CHART STARTS WITH THE PARENTS OF 195.

9th GENERATION	10th GENERATION	11th GENERATION	12th GENERATION
THEIR FATHER	NAME	NAME	NAME
NAME	BORN	BORN	LIVED
BORN	DIED	DIED	NAME
DIED	MARRIED	MARRIED	LIVED
MARRIED	NOTES	NAME	NAME
NOTES		BORN	LIVED
		DIED	NAME
		NOTES	LIVED
	NAME	NAME	NAME
	BORN	BORN	LIVED
	DIED	DIED	NAME
	NOTES	MARRIED	LIVED
		NAME	NAME
		BORN	LIVED
		DIED	NAME
		NOTES	LIVED
THEIR MOTHER	NAME	NAME	NAME
NAME	BORN	BORN	LIVED
BORN	DIED	DIED	NAME
DIED	MARRIED	MARRIED	LIVED
NOTES	NOTES	NAME	NAME
		BORN	LIVED
		DIED	NAME
		NOTES	LIVED
	NAME	NAME	NAME
	BORN	BORN	LIVED
	DIED	DIED	NAME
	NOTES	MARRIED	LIVED
		NAME	NAME
		BORN	LIVED
		DIED	NAME
		NOTES	LIVED

| 6X GREAT-GRANDPARENTS | 7X GREAT-GRANDPARENTS | 8X GREAT-GRANDPARENTS | 9X GREAT-GRANDPARENTS |

THIS CHART STARTS WITH THE PARENTS OF 196.

9th GENERATION	10th GENERATION	11th GENERATION	12th GENERATION
THEIR FATHER	NAME	NAME	NAME
NAME	BORN	BORN	LIVED
BORN	DIED	DIED	NAME
DIED	MARRIED	MARRIED	LIVED
MARRIED	NOTES	NAME	NAME
NOTES		BORN	LIVED
		DIED	NAME
		NOTES	LIVED
	NAME	NAME	NAME
	BORN	BORN	LIVED
	DIED	DIED	NAME
	NOTES	MARRIED	LIVED
		NAME	NAME
		BORN	LIVED
		DIED	NAME
		NOTES	LIVED
THEIR MOTHER	NAME	NAME	NAME
NAME	BORN	BORN	LIVED
BORN	DIED	DIED	NAME
DIED	MARRIED	MARRIED	LIVED
NOTES	NOTES	NAME	NAME
		BORN	LIVED
		DIED	NAME
		NOTES	LIVED
	NAME	NAME	NAME
	BORN	BORN	LIVED
	DIED	DIED	NAME
	NOTES	MARRIED	LIVED
		NAME	NAME
		BORN	LIVED
		DIED	NAME
		NOTES	LIVED

| 6X GREAT-GRANDPARENTS | 7X GREAT-GRANDPARENTS | 8X GREAT-GRANDPARENTS | 9X GREAT-GRANDPARENTS |

9th GENERATION	10th GENERATION	11th GENERATION	12th GENERATION
THEIR FATHER	NAME	NAME	NAME
NAME	BORN	BORN	LIVED
BORN	DIED	DIED	NAME
DIED	MARRIED	MARRIED	LIVED
MARRIED	NOTES	NAME	NAME
NOTES		BORN	LIVED
		DIED	NAME
		NOTES	LIVED
	NAME	NAME	NAME
	BORN	BORN	LIVED
	DIED	DIED	NAME
	NOTES	MARRIED	LIVED
		NAME	NAME
		BORN	LIVED
		DIED	NAME
		NOTES	LIVED
THEIR MOTHER	NAME	NAME	NAME
NAME	BORN	BORN	LIVED
BORN	DIED	DIED	NAME
DIED	MARRIED	MARRIED	LIVED
NOTES	NOTES	NAME	NAME
		BORN	LIVED
		DIED	NAME
		NOTES	LIVED
	NAME	NAME	NAME
	BORN	BORN	LIVED
	DIED	DIED	NAME
	NOTES	MARRIED	LIVED
		NAME	NAME
		BORN	LIVED
		DIED	NAME
		NOTES	LIVED

6X GREAT-GRANDPARENTS	7X GREAT-GRANDPARENTS	8X GREAT-GRANDPARENTS	9X GREAT-GRANDPARENTS

THIS CHART STARTS WITH THE PARENTS OF 198_

9th GENERATION	10th GENERATION	11th GENERATION	12th GENERATION
THEIR FATHER	NAME	NAME	NAME
NAME	BORN	BORN	LIVED
BORN	DIED	DIED	NAME
DIED	MARRIED	MARRIED	LIVED
MARRIED	NOTES	NAME	NAME
NOTES		BORN	LIVED
		DIED	NAME
		NOTES	LIVED
	NAME	NAME	NAME
	BORN	BORN	LIVED
	DIED	DIED	NAME
	NOTES	MARRIED	LIVED
		NAME	NAME
		BORN	LIVED
		DIED	NAME
		NOTES	LIVED
THEIR MOTHER	NAME	NAME	NAME
NAME	BORN	BORN	LIVED
BORN	DIED	DIED	NAME
DIED	MARRIED	MARRIED	LIVED
NOTES	NOTES	NAME	NAME
		BORN	LIVED
		DIED	NAME
		NOTES	LIVED
	NAME	NAME	NAME
	BORN	BORN	LIVED
	DIED	DIED	NAME
	NOTES	MARRIED	LIVED
		NAME	NAME
		BORN	LIVED
		DIED	NAME
		NOTES	LIVED

6X GREAT-GRANDPARENTS	7X GREAT-GRANDPARENTS	8X GREAT-GRANDPARENTS	9X GREAT-GRANDPARENTS

THIS CHART STARTS WITH THE PARENTS OF 199.

9th GENERATION	10th GENERATION	11th GENERATION	12th GENERATION
THEIR FATHER	NAME	NAME	NAME
NAME	BORN	BORN	LIVED
BORN	DIED	DIED	NAME
DIED	MARRIED	MARRIED	LIVED
MARRIED	NOTES	NAME	NAME
NOTES		BORN	LIVED
		DIED	NAME
		NOTES	LIVED
	NAME	NAME	NAME
	BORN	BORN	LIVED
	DIED	DIED	NAME
	NOTES	MARRIED	LIVED
		NAME	NAME
		BORN	LIVED
		DIED	NAME
		NOTES	LIVED
THEIR MOTHER	NAME	NAME	NAME
NAME	BORN	BORN	LIVED
BORN	DIED	DIED	NAME
DIED	MARRIED	MARRIED	LIVED
NOTES	NOTES	NAME	NAME
		BORN	LIVED
		DIED	NAME
		NOTES	LIVED
	NAME	NAME	NAME
	BORN	BORN	LIVED
	DIED	DIED	NAME
	NOTES	MARRIED	LIVED
		NAME	NAME
		BORN	LIVED
		DIED	NAME
		NOTES	LIVED

6X GREAT-GRANDPARENTS	7X GREAT-GRANDPARENTS	8X GREAT-GRANDPARENTS	9X GREAT-GRANDPARENTS

9th GENERATION	10th GENERATION	11th GENERATION	12th GENERATION
THEIR FATHER	NAME	NAME	NAME
NAME	BORN	BORN	LIVED
BORN	DIED	DIED	NAME
DIED	MARRIED	MARRIED	LIVED
MARRIED	NOTES	NAME	NAME
NOTES		BORN	LIVED
		DIED	NAME
		NOTES	LIVED
	NAME	NAME	NAME
	BORN	BORN	LIVED
	DIED	DIED	NAME
	NOTES	MARRIED	LIVED
		NAME	NAME
		BORN	LIVED
		DIED	NAME
		NOTES	LIVED
THEIR MOTHER	NAME	NAME	NAME
NAME	BORN	BORN	LIVED
BORN	DIED	DIED	NAME
DIED	MARRIED	MARRIED	LIVED
NOTES	NOTES	NAME	NAME
		BORN	LIVED
		DIED	NAME
		NOTES	LIVED
	NAME	NAME	NAME
	BORN	BORN	LIVED
	DIED	DIED	NAME
	NOTES	MARRIED	LIVED
		NAME	NAME
		BORN	LIVED
		DIED	NAME
		NOTES	LIVED

6X GREAT-GRANDPARENTS	7X GREAT-GRANDPARENTS	8X GREAT-GRANDPARENTS	9X GREAT-GRANDPARENTS

9th GENERATION	10th GENERATION	11th GENERATION	12th GENERATION
THEIR FATHER	NAME	NAME	NAME
NAME	BORN	BORN	LIVED
BORN	DIED	DIED	NAME
DIED	MARRIED	MARRIED	LIVED
MARRIED	NOTES	NAME	NAME
NOTES		BORN	LIVED
		DIED	NAME
		NOTES	LIVED
	NAME	NAME	NAME
	BORN	BORN	LIVED
	DIED	DIED	NAME
	NOTES	MARRIED	LIVED
		NAME	NAME
		BORN	LIVED
		DIED	NAME
		NOTES	LIVED
THEIR MOTHER	NAME	NAME	NAME
NAME	BORN	BORN	LIVED
BORN	DIED	DIED	NAME
DIED	MARRIED	MARRIED	LIVED
NOTES	NOTES	NAME	NAME
		BORN	LIVED
		DIED	NAME
		NOTES	LIVED
	NAME	NAME	NAME
	BORN	BORN	LIVED
	DIED	DIED	NAME
	NOTES	MARRIED	LIVED
		NAME	NAME
		BORN	LIVED
		DIED	NAME
		NOTES	LIVED

6X GREAT-GRANDPARENTS	7X GREAT-GRANDPARENTS	8X GREAT-GRANDPARENTS	9X GREAT-GRANDPARENTS

THIS CHART STARTS WITH THE PARENTS OF 202.

9th GENERATION	10th GENERATION	11th GENERATION	12th GENERATION
THEIR FATHER	NAME	NAME	NAME
NAME	BORN	BORN	LIVED
BORN	DIED	DIED	NAME
DIED	MARRIED	MARRIED	LIVED
MARRIED	NOTES	NAME	NAME
NOTES		BORN	LIVED
		DIED	NAME
		NOTES	LIVED
	NAME	NAME	NAME
	BORN	BORN	LIVED
	DIED	DIED	NAME
	NOTES	MARRIED	LIVED
		NAME	NAME
		BORN	LIVED
		DIED	NAME
		NOTES	LIVED
THEIR MOTHER	NAME	NAME	NAME
NAME	BORN	BORN	LIVED
BORN	DIED	DIED	NAME
DIED	MARRIED	MARRIED	LIVED
NOTES	NOTES	NAME	NAME
		BORN	LIVED
		DIED	NAME
		NOTES	LIVED
	NAME	NAME	NAME
	BORN	BORN	LIVED
	DIED	DIED	NAME
	NOTES	MARRIED	LIVED
		NAME	NAME
		BORN	LIVED
		DIED	NAME
		NOTES	LIVED

6X GREAT-GRANDPARENTS	7X GREAT-GRANDPARENTS	8X GREAT-GRANDPARENTS	9X GREAT-GRANDPARENTS

9th GENERATION	10th GENERATION	11th GENERATION	12th GENERATION
THEIR FATHER	NAME	NAME	NAME
NAME	BORN	BORN	LIVED
BORN	DIED	DIED	NAME
DIED	MARRIED	MARRIED	LIVED
MARRIED	NOTES	NAME	NAME
NOTES		BORN	LIVED
		DIED	NAME
		NOTES	LIVED
	NAME	NAME	NAME
	BORN	BORN	LIVED
	DIED	DIED	NAME
	NOTES	MARRIED	LIVED
		NAME	NAME
		BORN	LIVED
		DIED	NAME
		NOTES	LIVED
THEIR MOTHER	NAME	NAME	NAME
NAME	BORN	BORN	LIVED
BORN	DIED	DIED	NAME
DIED	MARRIED	MARRIED	LIVED
NOTES	NOTES	NAME	NAME
		BORN	LIVED
		DIED	NAME
		NOTES	LIVED
	NAME	NAME	NAME
	BORN	BORN	LIVED
	DIED	DIED	NAME
	NOTES	MARRIED	LIVED
		NAME	NAME
		BORN	LIVED
		DIED	NAME
		NOTES	LIVED

6X GREAT-GRANDPARENTS	7X GREAT-GRANDPARENTS	8X GREAT-GRANDPARENTS	9X GREAT-GRANDPARENTS

9th GENERATION	10th GENERATION	11th GENERATION	12th GENERATION
THEIR FATHER	NAME	NAME	NAME
NAME	BORN	BORN	LIVED
BORN	DIED	DIED	NAME
DIED	MARRIED	MARRIED	LIVED
MARRIED	NOTES	NAME	NAME
NOTES		BORN	LIVED
		DIED	NAME
		NOTES	LIVED
	NAME	NAME	NAME
	BORN	BORN	LIVED
	DIED	DIED	NAME
	NOTES	MARRIED	LIVED
		NAME	NAME
		BORN	LIVED
		DIED	NAME
		NOTES	LIVED
THEIR MOTHER	NAME	NAME	NAME
NAME	BORN	BORN	LIVED
BORN	DIED	DIED	NAME
DIED	MARRIED	MARRIED	LIVED
NOTES	NOTES	NAME	NAME
		BORN	LIVED
		DIED	NAME
		NOTES	LIVED
	NAME	NAME	NAME
	BORN	BORN	LIVED
	DIED	DIED	NAME
	NOTES	MARRIED	LIVED
		NAME	NAME
		BORN	LIVED
		DIED	NAME
		NOTES	LIVED

| 6X GREAT-GRANDPARENTS | 7X GREAT-GRANDPARENTS | 8X GREAT-GRANDPARENTS | 9X GREAT-GRANDPARENTS |

THIS CHART STARTS WITH THE PARENTS OF 205.

9th GENERATION	10th GENERATION	11th GENERATION	12th GENERATION
THEIR FATHER	NAME	NAME	NAME
NAME	BORN	BORN	LIVED
BORN	DIED	DIED	NAME
DIED	MARRIED	MARRIED	LIVED
MARRIED	NOTES	NAME	NAME
NOTES		BORN	LIVED
		DIED	NAME
		NOTES	LIVED
	NAME	NAME	NAME
	BORN	BORN	LIVED
	DIED	DIED	NAME
	NOTES	MARRIED	LIVED
		NAME	NAME
		BORN	LIVED
		DIED	NAME
		NOTES	LIVED
THEIR MOTHER	NAME	NAME	NAME
NAME	BORN	BORN	LIVED
BORN	DIED	DIED	NAME
DIED	MARRIED	MARRIED	LIVED
NOTES	NOTES	NAME	NAME
		BORN	LIVED
		DIED	NAME
		NOTES	LIVED
	NAME	NAME	NAME
	BORN	BORN	LIVED
	DIED	DIED	NAME
	NOTES	MARRIED	LIVED
		NAME	NAME
		BORN	LIVED
		DIED	NAME
		NOTES	LIVED

| 6X GREAT-GRANDPARENTS | 7X GREAT-GRANDPARENTS | 8X GREAT-GRANDPARENTS | 9X GREAT-GRANDPARENTS |

THIS CHART STARTS WITH THE PARENTS OF 206.

9th GENERATION	10th GENERATION	11th GENERATION	12th GENERATION
THEIR FATHER	NAME	NAME	NAME
NAME	BORN	BORN	LIVED
BORN	DIED	DIED	NAME
DIED	MARRIED	MARRIED	LIVED
MARRIED	NOTES	NAME	NAME
NOTES		BORN	LIVED
		DIED	NAME
		NOTES	LIVED
	NAME	NAME	NAME
	BORN	BORN	LIVED
	DIED	DIED	NAME
	NOTES	MARRIED	LIVED
		NAME	NAME
		BORN	LIVED
		DIED	NAME
		NOTES	LIVED
THEIR MOTHER	NAME	NAME	NAME
NAME	BORN	BORN	LIVED
BORN	DIED	DIED	NAME
DIED	MARRIED	MARRIED	LIVED
NOTES	NOTES	NAME	NAME
		BORN	LIVED
		DIED	NAME
		NOTES	LIVED
	NAME	NAME	NAME
	BORN	BORN	LIVED
	DIED	DIED	NAME
	NOTES	MARRIED	LIVED
		NAME	NAME
		BORN	LIVED
		DIED	NAME
		NOTES	LIVED

6X GREAT-GRANDPARENTS	7X GREAT-GRANDPARENTS	8X GREAT-GRANDPARENTS	9X GREAT-GRANDPARENTS

9th GENERATION	10th GENERATION	11th GENERATION	12th GENERATION
THEIR FATHER	NAME	NAME	NAME
NAME	BORN	BORN	LIVED
BORN	DIED	DIED	NAME
DIED	MARRIED	MARRIED	LIVED
MARRIED	NOTES	NAME	NAME
NOTES		BORN	LIVED
		DIED	NAME
		NOTES	LIVED
	NAME	NAME	NAME
	BORN	BORN	LIVED
	DIED	DIED	NAME
	NOTES	MARRIED	LIVED
		NAME	NAME
		BORN	LIVED
		DIED	NAME
		NOTES	LIVED
THEIR MOTHER	NAME	NAME	NAME
NAME	BORN	BORN	LIVED
BORN	DIED	DIED	NAME
DIED	MARRIED	MARRIED	LIVED
NOTES	NOTES	NAME	NAME
		BORN	LIVED
		DIED	NAME
		NOTES	LIVED
	NAME	NAME	NAME
	BORN	BORN	LIVED
	DIED	DIED	NAME
	NOTES	MARRIED	LIVED
		NAME	NAME
		BORN	LIVED
		DIED	NAME
		NOTES	LIVED

THIS CHART STARTS WITH THE PARENTS OF 208.

9th GENERATION	10th GENERATION	11th GENERATION	12th GENERATION
THEIR FATHER	NAME	NAME	NAME
NAME	BORN	BORN	LIVED
BORN	DIED	DIED	NAME
DIED	MARRIED	MARRIED	LIVED
MARRIED	NOTES	NAME	NAME
NOTES		BORN	LIVED
		DIED	NAME
		NOTES	LIVED
	NAME	NAME	NAME
	BORN	BORN	LIVED
	DIED	DIED	NAME
	NOTES	MARRIED	LIVED
		NAME	NAME
		BORN	LIVED
		DIED	NAME
		NOTES	LIVED
THEIR MOTHER	NAME	NAME	NAME
NAME	BORN	BORN	LIVED
BORN	DIED	DIED	NAME
DIED	MARRIED	MARRIED	LIVED
NOTES	NOTES	NAME	NAME
		BORN	LIVED
		DIED	NAME
		NOTES	LIVED
	NAME	NAME	NAME
	BORN	BORN	LIVED
	DIED	DIED	NAME
	NOTES	MARRIED	LIVED
		NAME	NAME
		BORN	LIVED
		DIED	NAME
		NOTES	LIVED

| 6X GREAT-GRANDPARENTS | 7X GREAT-GRANDPARENTS | 8X GREAT-GRANDPARENTS | 9X GREAT-GRANDPARENTS |

9th GENERATION	10th GENERATION	11th GENERATION	12th GENERATION
THEIR FATHER	NAME	NAME	NAME
NAME	BORN	BORN	LIVED
BORN	DIED	DIED	NAME
DIED	MARRIED	MARRIED	LIVED
MARRIED	NOTES	NAME	NAME
NOTES		BORN	LIVED
		DIED	NAME
		NOTES	LIVED
	NAME	NAME	NAME
	BORN	BORN	LIVED
	DIED	DIED	NAME
	NOTES	MARRIED	LIVED
		NAME	NAME
		BORN	LIVED
		DIED	NAME
		NOTES	LIVED
THEIR MOTHER	NAME	NAME	NAME
NAME	BORN	BORN	LIVED
BORN	DIED	DIED	NAME
DIED	MARRIED	MARRIED	LIVED
NOTES	NOTES	NAME	NAME
		BORN	LIVED
		DIED	NAME
		NOTES	LIVED
	NAME	NAME	NAME
	BORN	BORN	LIVED
	DIED	DIED	NAME
	NOTES	MARRIED	LIVED
		NAME	NAME
		BORN	LIVED
		DIED	NAME
		NOTES	LIVED

6X GREAT-GRANDPARENTS	7X GREAT-GRANDPARENTS	8X GREAT-GRANDPARENTS	9X GREAT-GRANDPARENTS

9th GENERATION	10th GENERATION	11th GENERATION	12th GENERATION
THEIR FATHER	NAME	NAME	NAME
NAME	BORN	BORN	LIVED
BORN	DIED	DIED	NAME
DIED	MARRIED	MARRIED	LIVED
MARRIED	NOTES	NAME	NAME
NOTES		BORN	LIVED
		DIED	NAME
		NOTES	LIVED
	NAME	NAME	NAME
	BORN	BORN	LIVED
	DIED	DIED	NAME
	NOTES	MARRIED	LIVED
		NAME	NAME
		BORN	LIVED
		DIED	NAME
		NOTES	LIVED
THEIR MOTHER	NAME	NAME	NAME
NAME	BORN	BORN	LIVED
BORN	DIED	DIED	NAME
DIED	MARRIED	MARRIED	LIVED
NOTES	NOTES	NAME	NAME
		BORN	LIVED
		DIED	NAME
		NOTES	LIVED
	NAME	NAME	NAME
	BORN	BORN	LIVED
	DIED	DIED	NAME
	NOTES	MARRIED	LIVED
		NAME	NAME
		BORN	LIVED
		DIED	NAME
		NOTES	LIVED

6X GREAT-GRANDPARENTS	7X GREAT-GRANDPARENTS	8X GREAT-GRANDPARENTS	9X GREAT-GRANDPARENTS

THIS CHART STARTS WITH THE PARENTS OF 211.

9th GENERATION	10th GENERATION	11th GENERATION	12th GENERATION
THEIR FATHER	NAME	NAME	NAME
NAME	BORN	BORN	LIVED
BORN	DIED	DIED	NAME
DIED	MARRIED	MARRIED	LIVED
MARRIED	NOTES	NAME	NAME
NOTES		BORN	LIVED
		DIED	NAME
		NOTES	LIVED
	NAME	NAME	NAME
	BORN	BORN	LIVED
	DIED	DIED	NAME
	NOTES	MARRIED	LIVED
		NAME	NAME
		BORN	LIVED
		DIED	NAME
		NOTES	LIVED
THEIR MOTHER	NAME	NAME	NAME
NAME	BORN	BORN	LIVED
BORN	DIED	DIED	NAME
DIED	MARRIED	MARRIED	LIVED
NOTES	NOTES	NAME	NAME
		BORN	LIVED
		DIED	NAME
		NOTES	LIVED
	NAME	NAME	NAME
	BORN	BORN	LIVED
	DIED	DIED	NAME
	NOTES	MARRIED	LIVED
		NAME	NAME
		BORN	LIVED
		DIED	NAME
		NOTES	LIVED

6X GREAT-GRANDPARENTS	7X GREAT-GRANDPARENTS	8X GREAT-GRANDPARENTS	9X GREAT-GRANDPARENTS

THIS CHART STARTS WITH THE PARENTS OF 212.

9th GENERATION	10th GENERATION	11th GENERATION	12th GENERATION
THEIR FATHER	NAME	NAME	NAME
NAME	BORN	BORN	LIVED
BORN	DIED	DIED	NAME
DIED	MARRIED	MARRIED	LIVED
MARRIED	NOTES	NAME	NAME
NOTES		BORN	LIVED
		DIED	NAME
		NOTES	LIVED
	NAME	NAME	NAME
	BORN	BORN	LIVED
	DIED	DIED	NAME
	NOTES	MARRIED	LIVED
		NAME	NAME
		BORN	LIVED
		DIED	NAME
		NOTES	LIVED
THEIR MOTHER	NAME	NAME	NAME
NAME	BORN	BORN	LIVED
BORN	DIED	DIED	NAME
DIED	MARRIED	MARRIED	LIVED
NOTES	NOTES	NAME	NAME
		BORN	LIVED
		DIED	NAME
		NOTES	LIVED
	NAME	NAME	NAME
	BORN	BORN	LIVED
	DIED	DIED	NAME
	NOTES	MARRIED	LIVED
		NAME	NAME
		BORN	LIVED
		DIED	NAME
		NOTES	LIVED

| 6X GREAT-GRANDPARENTS | 7X GREAT-GRANDPARENTS | 8X GREAT-GRANDPARENTS | 9X GREAT-GRANDPARENTS |

9th GENERATION	10th GENERATION	11th GENERATION	12th GENERATION
THEIR FATHER	NAME	NAME	NAME
NAME	BORN	BORN	LIVED
BORN	DIED	DIED	NAME
DIED	MARRIED	MARRIED	LIVED
MARRIED	NOTES	NAME	NAME
NOTES		BORN	LIVED
		DIED	NAME
		NOTES	LIVED
	NAME	NAME	NAME
	BORN	BORN	LIVED
	DIED	DIED	NAME
	NOTES	MARRIED	LIVED
		NAME	NAME
		BORN	LIVED
		DIED	NAME
		NOTES	LIVED
THEIR MOTHER	NAME	NAME	NAME
NAME	BORN	BORN	LIVED
BORN	DIED	DIED	NAME
DIED	MARRIED	MARRIED	LIVED
NOTES	NOTES	NAME	NAME
		BORN	LIVED
		DIED	NAME
		NOTES	LIVED
	NAME	NAME	NAME
	BORN	BORN	LIVED
	DIED	DIED	NAME
	NOTES	MARRIED	LIVED
		NAME	NAME
		BORN	LIVED
		DIED	NAME
		NOTES	LIVED

6X GREAT-GRANDPARENTS	7X GREAT-GRANDPARENTS	8X GREAT-GRANDPARENTS	9X GREAT-GRANDPARENTS

THIS CHART STARTS WITH THE PARENTS OF 214.

9th GENERATION	10th GENERATION	11th GENERATION	12th GENERATION
THEIR FATHER NAME BORN DIED MARRIED NOTES	NAME BORN DIED MARRIED NOTES	NAME BORN DIED MARRIED	NAME LIVED
			NAME LIVED
		NAME BORN DIED NOTES	NAME LIVED
			NAME LIVED
			NAME LIVED
	NAME BORN DIED NOTES	NAME BORN DIED MARRIED	NAME LIVED
			NAME LIVED
		NAME BORN DIED NOTES	NAME LIVED
			NAME LIVED
			NAME LIVED
THEIR MOTHER NAME BORN DIED NOTES	NAME BORN DIED MARRIED NOTES	NAME BORN DIED MARRIED	NAME LIVED
			NAME LIVED
		NAME BORN DIED NOTES	NAME LIVED
			NAME LIVED
			NAME LIVED
	NAME BORN DIED NOTES	NAME BORN DIED MARRIED	NAME LIVED
			NAME LIVED
		NAME BORN DIED NOTES	NAME LIVED
			NAME LIVED
			NAME LIVED
6X GREAT-GRANDPARENTS	7X GREAT-GRANDPARENTS	8X GREAT-GRANDPARENTS	9X GREAT-GRANDPARENTS

9th GENERATION	10th GENERATION	11th GENERATION	12th GENERATION
THEIR FATHER	NAME	NAME	NAME
NAME	BORN	BORN	LIVED
BORN	DIED	DIED	NAME
DIED	MARRIED	MARRIED	LIVED
MARRIED	NOTES	NAME	NAME
NOTES		BORN	LIVED
		DIED	NAME
		NOTES	LIVED
	NAME	NAME	NAME
	BORN	BORN	LIVED
	DIED	DIED	NAME
	NOTES	MARRIED	LIVED
		NAME	NAME
		BORN	LIVED
		DIED	NAME
		NOTES	LIVED
THEIR MOTHER	NAME	NAME	NAME
NAME	BORN	BORN	LIVED
BORN	DIED	DIED	NAME
DIED	MARRIED	MARRIED	LIVED
NOTES	NOTES	NAME	NAME
		BORN	LIVED
		DIED	NAME
		NOTES	LIVED
	NAME	NAME	NAME
	BORN	BORN	LIVED
	DIED	DIED	NAME
	NOTES	MARRIED	LIVED
		NAME	NAME
		BORN	LIVED
		DIED	NAME
		NOTES	LIVED

6X GREAT-GRANDPARENTS	7X GREAT-GRANDPARENTS	8X GREAT-GRANDPARENTS	9X GREAT-GRANDPARENTS

9th GENERATION	10th GENERATION	11th GENERATION	12th GENERATION
THEIR FATHER	NAME	NAME	NAME
NAME	BORN	BORN	LIVED
BORN	DIED	DIED	NAME
DIED	MARRIED	MARRIED	LIVED
MARRIED	NOTES	NAME	NAME
NOTES		BORN	LIVED
		DIED	NAME
		NOTES	LIVED
	NAME	NAME	NAME
	BORN	BORN	LIVED
	DIED	DIED	NAME
	NOTES	MARRIED	LIVED
		NAME	NAME
		BORN	LIVED
		DIED	NAME
		NOTES	LIVED
THEIR MOTHER	NAME	NAME	NAME
NAME	BORN	BORN	LIVED
BORN	DIED	DIED	NAME
DIED	MARRIED	MARRIED	LIVED
NOTES	NOTES	NAME	NAME
		BORN	LIVED
		DIED	NAME
		NOTES	LIVED
	NAME	NAME	NAME
	BORN	BORN	LIVED
	DIED	DIED	NAME
	NOTES	MARRIED	LIVED
		NAME	NAME
		BORN	LIVED
		DIED	NAME
		NOTES	LIVED

6X GREAT-GRANDPARENTS	7X GREAT-GRANDPARENTS	8X GREAT-GRANDPARENTS	9X GREAT-GRANDPARENTS

9th GENERATION	10th GENERATION	11th GENERATION	12th GENERATION
THEIR FATHER	NAME	NAME	NAME
NAME	BORN	BORN	LIVED
BORN	DIED	DIED	NAME
DIED	MARRIED	MARRIED	LIVED
MARRIED	NOTES	NAME	NAME
NOTES		BORN	LIVED
		DIED	NAME
		NOTES	LIVED
	NAME	NAME	NAME
	BORN	BORN	LIVED
	DIED	DIED	NAME
	NOTES	MARRIED	LIVED
		NAME	NAME
		BORN	LIVED
		DIED	NAME
		NOTES	LIVED
THEIR MOTHER	NAME	NAME	NAME
NAME	BORN	BORN	LIVED
BORN	DIED	DIED	NAME
DIED	MARRIED	MARRIED	LIVED
NOTES	NOTES	NAME	NAME
		BORN	LIVED
		DIED	NAME
		NOTES	LIVED
	NAME	NAME	NAME
	BORN	BORN	LIVED
	DIED	DIED	NAME
	NOTES	MARRIED	LIVED
		NAME	NAME
		BORN	LIVED
		DIED	NAME
		NOTES	LIVED

6X GREAT-GRANDPARENTS	7X GREAT-GRANDPARENTS	8X GREAT-GRANDPARENTS	9X GREAT-GRANDPARENTS

THIS CHART STARTS WITH THE PARENTS OF 218.

9th GENERATION	10th GENERATION	11th GENERATION	12th GENERATION
THEIR FATHER	NAME	NAME	NAME
NAME	BORN	BORN	LIVED
BORN	DIED	DIED	NAME
DIED	MARRIED	MARRIED	LIVED
MARRIED	NOTES	NAME	NAME
NOTES		BORN	LIVED
		DIED	NAME
		NOTES	LIVED
	NAME	NAME	NAME
	BORN	BORN	LIVED
	DIED	DIED	NAME
	NOTES	MARRIED	LIVED
		NAME	NAME
		BORN	LIVED
		DIED	NAME
		NOTES	LIVED
THEIR MOTHER	NAME	NAME	NAME
NAME	BORN	BORN	LIVED
BORN	DIED	DIED	NAME
DIED	MARRIED	MARRIED	LIVED
NOTES	NOTES	NAME	NAME
		BORN	LIVED
		DIED	NAME
		NOTES	LIVED
	NAME	NAME	NAME
	BORN	BORN	LIVED
	DIED	DIED	NAME
	NOTES	MARRIED	LIVED
		NAME	NAME
		BORN	LIVED
		DIED	NAME
		NOTES	LIVED

6X GREAT-GRANDPARENTS	7X GREAT-GRANDPARENTS	8X GREAT-GRANDPARENTS	9X GREAT-GRANDPARENTS

THIS CHART STARTS WITH THE PARENTS OF 219.

9th GENERATION	10th GENERATION	11th GENERATION	12th GENERATION
THEIR FATHER	NAME	NAME	NAME
NAME	BORN	BORN	LIVED
BORN	DIED	DIED	NAME
DIED	MARRIED	MARRIED	LIVED
MARRIED	NOTES	NAME	NAME
NOTES		BORN	LIVED
		DIED	NAME
		NOTES	LIVED
	NAME	NAME	NAME
	BORN	BORN	LIVED
	DIED	DIED	NAME
	NOTES	MARRIED	LIVED
		NAME	NAME
		BORN	LIVED
		DIED	NAME
		NOTES	LIVED
THEIR MOTHER	NAME	NAME	NAME
NAME	BORN	BORN	LIVED
BORN	DIED	DIED	NAME
DIED	MARRIED	MARRIED	LIVED
NOTES	NOTES	NAME	NAME
		BORN	LIVED
		DIED	NAME
		NOTES	LIVED
	NAME	NAME	NAME
	BORN	BORN	LIVED
	DIED	DIED	NAME
	NOTES	MARRIED	LIVED
		NAME	NAME
		BORN	LIVED
		DIED	NAME
		NOTES	LIVED

| 6X GREAT-GRANDPARENTS | 7X GREAT-GRANDPARENTS | 8X GREAT-GRANDPARENTS | 9X GREAT-GRANDPARENTS |

THIS CHART STARTS WITH THE PARENTS OF 220.

9th GENERATION	10th GENERATION	11th GENERATION	12th GENERATION
THEIR FATHER	NAME	NAME	NAME
NAME	BORN	BORN	LIVED
BORN	DIED	DIED	NAME
DIED	MARRIED	MARRIED	LIVED
MARRIED	NOTES	NAME	NAME
NOTES		BORN	LIVED
		DIED	NAME
		NOTES	LIVED
	NAME	NAME	NAME
	BORN	BORN	LIVED
	DIED	DIED	NAME
	NOTES	MARRIED	LIVED
		NAME	NAME
		BORN	LIVED
		DIED	NAME
		NOTES	LIVED
THEIR MOTHER	NAME	NAME	NAME
NAME	BORN	BORN	LIVED
BORN	DIED	DIED	NAME
DIED	MARRIED	MARRIED	LIVED
NOTES	NOTES	NAME	NAME
		BORN	LIVED
		DIED	NAME
		NOTES	LIVED
	NAME	NAME	NAME
	BORN	BORN	LIVED
	DIED	DIED	NAME
	NOTES	MARRIED	LIVED
		NAME	NAME
		BORN	LIVED
		DIED	NAME
		NOTES	LIVED

6X GREAT-GRANDPARENTS	7X GREAT-GRANDPARENTS	8X GREAT-GRANDPARENTS	9X GREAT-GRANDPARENTS

9th GENERATION	10th GENERATION	11th GENERATION	12th GENERATION
THEIR FATHER	NAME	NAME	NAME
NAME	BORN	BORN	LIVED
BORN	DIED	DIED	NAME
DIED	MARRIED	MARRIED	LIVED
MARRIED	NOTES	NAME	NAME
NOTES		BORN	LIVED
		DIED	NAME
		NOTES	LIVED
	NAME	NAME	NAME
	BORN	BORN	LIVED
	DIED	DIED	NAME
	NOTES	MARRIED	LIVED
		NAME	NAME
		BORN	LIVED
		DIED	NAME
		NOTES	LIVED
THEIR MOTHER	NAME	NAME	NAME
NAME	BORN	BORN	LIVED
BORN	DIED	DIED	NAME
DIED	MARRIED	MARRIED	LIVED
NOTES	NOTES	NAME	NAME
		BORN	LIVED
		DIED	NAME
		NOTES	LIVED
	NAME	NAME	NAME
	BORN	BORN	LIVED
	DIED	DIED	NAME
	NOTES	MARRIED	LIVED
		NAME	NAME
		BORN	LIVED
		DIED	NAME
		NOTES	LIVED

| 6X GREAT-GRANDPARENTS | 7X GREAT-GRANDPARENTS | 8X GREAT-GRANDPARENTS | 9X GREAT-GRANDPARENTS |

THIS CHART STARTS WITH THE PARENTS OF 222.

9th GENERATION	10th GENERATION	11th GENERATION	12th GENERATION
THEIR FATHER	NAME	NAME	NAME
NAME	BORN	BORN	LIVED
BORN	DIED	DIED	NAME
DIED	MARRIED	MARRIED	LIVED
MARRIED	NOTES	NAME	NAME
NOTES		BORN	LIVED
		DIED	NAME
		NOTES	LIVED
	NAME	NAME	NAME
	BORN	BORN	LIVED
	DIED	DIED	NAME
	NOTES	MARRIED	LIVED
		NAME	NAME
		BORN	LIVED
		DIED	NAME
		NOTES	LIVED
THEIR MOTHER	NAME	NAME	NAME
NAME	BORN	BORN	LIVED
BORN	DIED	DIED	NAME
DIED	MARRIED	MARRIED	LIVED
NOTES	NOTES	NAME	NAME
		BORN	LIVED
		DIED	NAME
		NOTES	LIVED
	NAME	NAME	NAME
	BORN	BORN	LIVED
	DIED	DIED	NAME
	NOTES	MARRIED	LIVED
		NAME	NAME
		BORN	LIVED
		DIED	NAME
		NOTES	LIVED

9th GENERATION	10th GENERATION	11th GENERATION	12th GENERATION
THEIR FATHER	NAME	NAME	NAME
NAME	BORN	BORN	LIVED
BORN	DIED	DIED	NAME
DIED	MARRIED	MARRIED	LIVED
MARRIED	NOTES	NAME	NAME
NOTES		BORN	LIVED
		DIED	NAME
		NOTES	LIVED
	NAME	NAME	NAME
	BORN	BORN	LIVED
	DIED	DIED	NAME
	NOTES	MARRIED	LIVED
		NAME	NAME
		BORN	LIVED
		DIED	NAME
		NOTES	LIVED
THEIR MOTHER	NAME	NAME	NAME
NAME	BORN	BORN	LIVED
BORN	DIED	DIED	NAME
DIED	MARRIED	MARRIED	LIVED
NOTES	NOTES	NAME	NAME
		BORN	LIVED
		DIED	NAME
		NOTES	LIVED
	NAME	NAME	NAME
	BORN	BORN	LIVED
	DIED	DIED	NAME
	NOTES	MARRIED	LIVED
		NAME	NAME
		BORN	LIVED
		DIED	NAME
		NOTES	LIVED

6X GREAT-GRANDPARENTS	7X GREAT-GRANDPARENTS	8X GREAT-GRANDPARENTS	9X GREAT-GRANDPARENTS

9th GENERATION	10th GENERATION	11th GENERATION	12th GENERATION
THEIR FATHER	NAME	NAME	NAME
NAME	BORN	BORN	LIVED
BORN	DIED	DIED	NAME
DIED	MARRIED	MARRIED	LIVED
MARRIED	NOTES	NAME	NAME
NOTES		BORN	LIVED
		DIED	NAME
		NOTES	LIVED
	NAME	NAME	NAME
	BORN	BORN	LIVED
	DIED	DIED	NAME
	NOTES	MARRIED	LIVED
		NAME	NAME
		BORN	LIVED
		DIED	NAME
		NOTES	LIVED
THEIR MOTHER	NAME	NAME	NAME
NAME	BORN	BORN	LIVED
BORN	DIED	DIED	NAME
DIED	MARRIED	MARRIED	LIVED
NOTES	NOTES	NAME	NAME
		BORN	LIVED
		DIED	NAME
		NOTES	LIVED
	NAME	NAME	NAME
	BORN	BORN	LIVED
	DIED	DIED	NAME
	NOTES	MARRIED	LIVED
		NAME	NAME
		BORN	LIVED
		DIED	NAME
		NOTES	LIVED

6X GREAT-GRANDPARENTS	7X GREAT-GRANDPARENTS	8X GREAT-GRANDPARENTS	9X GREAT-GRANDPARENTS

THIS CHART STARTS WITH THE PARENTS OF 225

9th GENERATION	10th GENERATION	11th GENERATION	12th GENERATION
THEIR FATHER	NAME	NAME	NAME
NAME	BORN	BORN	LIVED
BORN	DIED	DIED	NAME
DIED	MARRIED	MARRIED	LIVED
MARRIED	NOTES	NAME	NAME
NOTES		BORN	LIVED
		DIED	NAME
		NOTES	LIVED
	NAME	NAME	NAME
	BORN	BORN	LIVED
	DIED	DIED	NAME
	NOTES	MARRIED	LIVED
		NAME	NAME
		BORN	LIVED
		DIED	NAME
		NOTES	LIVED
THEIR MOTHER	NAME	NAME	NAME
NAME	BORN	BORN	LIVED
BORN	DIED	DIED	NAME
DIED	MARRIED	MARRIED	LIVED
NOTES	NOTES	NAME	NAME
		BORN	LIVED
		DIED	NAME
		NOTES	LIVED
	NAME	NAME	NAME
	BORN	BORN	LIVED
	DIED	DIED	NAME
	NOTES	MARRIED	LIVED
		NAME	NAME
		BORN	LIVED
		DIED	NAME
		NOTES	LIVED

| 6X GREAT-GRANDPARENTS | 7X GREAT-GRANDPARENTS | 8X GREAT-GRANDPARENTS | 9X GREAT-GRANDPARENTS |

THIS CHART STARTS WITH THE PARENTS OF 226.

9th GENERATION	10th GENERATION	11th GENERATION	12th GENERATION
THEIR FATHER	NAME	NAME	NAME
NAME	BORN	BORN	LIVED
BORN	DIED	DIED	NAME
DIED	MARRIED	MARRIED	LIVED
MARRIED	NOTES	NAME	NAME
NOTES		BORN	LIVED
		DIED	NAME
		NOTES	LIVED
	NAME	NAME	NAME
	BORN	BORN	LIVED
	DIED	DIED	NAME
	NOTES	MARRIED	LIVED
		NAME	NAME
		BORN	LIVED
		DIED	NAME
		NOTES	LIVED
THEIR MOTHER	NAME	NAME	NAME
NAME	BORN	BORN	LIVED
BORN	DIED	DIED	NAME
DIED	MARRIED	MARRIED	LIVED
NOTES	NOTES	NAME	NAME
		BORN	LIVED
		DIED	NAME
		NOTES	LIVED
	NAME	NAME	NAME
	BORN	BORN	LIVED
	DIED	DIED	NAME
	NOTES	MARRIED	LIVED
		NAME	NAME
		BORN	LIVED
		DIED	NAME
		NOTES	LIVED

6X GREAT-GRANDPARENTS 7X GREAT-GRANDPARENTS 8X GREAT-GRANDPARENTS 9X GREAT-GRANDPARENTS

9th GENERATION	10th GENERATION	11th GENERATION	12th GENERATION
THEIR FATHER	NAME	NAME	NAME
NAME	BORN	BORN	LIVED
BORN	DIED	DIED	NAME
DIED	MARRIED	MARRIED	LIVED
MARRIED	NOTES	NAME	NAME
NOTES		BORN	LIVED
		DIED	NAME
		NOTES	LIVED
	NAME	NAME	NAME
	BORN	BORN	LIVED
	DIED	DIED	NAME
	NOTES	MARRIED	LIVED
		NAME	NAME
		BORN	LIVED
		DIED	NAME
		NOTES	LIVED
THEIR MOTHER	NAME	NAME	NAME
NAME	BORN	BORN	LIVED
BORN	DIED	DIED	NAME
DIED	MARRIED	MARRIED	LIVED
NOTES	NOTES	NAME	NAME
		BORN	LIVED
		DIED	NAME
		NOTES	LIVED
	NAME	NAME	NAME
	BORN	BORN	LIVED
	DIED	DIED	NAME
	NOTES	MARRIED	LIVED
		NAME	NAME
		BORN	LIVED
		DIED	NAME
		NOTES	LIVED

6X GREAT-GRANDPARENTS	7X GREAT-GRANDPARENTS	8X GREAT-GRANDPARENTS	9X GREAT-GRANDPARENTS

THIS CHART STARTS WITH THE PARENTS OF 228.

9th GENERATION	10th GENERATION	11th GENERATION	12th GENERATION
THEIR FATHER	NAME	NAME	NAME
NAME	BORN	BORN	LIVED
BORN	DIED	DIED	NAME
DIED	MARRIED	MARRIED	LIVED
MARRIED	NOTES	NAME	NAME
NOTES		BORN	LIVED
		DIED	NAME
		NOTES	LIVED
	NAME	NAME	NAME
	BORN	BORN	LIVED
	DIED	DIED	NAME
	NOTES	MARRIED	LIVED
		NAME	NAME
		BORN	LIVED
		DIED	NAME
		NOTES	LIVED
THEIR MOTHER	NAME	NAME	NAME
NAME	BORN	BORN	LIVED
BORN	DIED	DIED	NAME
DIED	MARRIED	MARRIED	LIVED
NOTES	NOTES	NAME	NAME
		BORN	LIVED
		DIED	NAME
		NOTES	LIVED
	NAME	NAME	NAME
	BORN	BORN	LIVED
	DIED	DIED	NAME
	NOTES	MARRIED	LIVED
		NAME	NAME
		BORN	LIVED
		DIED	NAME
		NOTES	LIVED

6X GREAT-GRANDPARENTS	7X GREAT-GRANDPARENTS	8X GREAT-GRANDPARENTS	9X GREAT-GRANDPARENTS

9th GENERATION	10th GENERATION	11th GENERATION	12th GENERATION
THEIR FATHER	NAME	NAME	NAME
NAME	BORN	BORN	LIVED
BORN	DIED	DIED	NAME
DIED	MARRIED	MARRIED	LIVED
MARRIED	NOTES	NAME	NAME
NOTES		BORN	LIVED
		DIED	NAME
		NOTES	LIVED
	NAME	NAME	NAME
	BORN	BORN	LIVED
	DIED	DIED	NAME
	NOTES	MARRIED	LIVED
		NAME	NAME
		BORN	LIVED
		DIED	NAME
		NOTES	LIVED
THEIR MOTHER	NAME	NAME	NAME
NAME	BORN	BORN	LIVED
BORN	DIED	DIED	NAME
DIED	MARRIED	MARRIED	LIVED
NOTES	NOTES	NAME	NAME
		BORN	LIVED
		DIED	NAME
		NOTES	LIVED
	NAME	NAME	NAME
	BORN	BORN	LIVED
	DIED	DIED	NAME
	NOTES	MARRIED	LIVED
		NAME	NAME
		BORN	LIVED
		DIED	NAME
		NOTES	LIVED

6X GREAT-GRANDPARENTS	7X GREAT-GRANDPARENTS	8X GREAT-GRANDPARENTS	9X GREAT-GRANDPARENTS

THIS CHART STARTS WITH THE PARENTS OF 230.

9th GENERATION	10th GENERATION	11th GENERATION	12th GENERATION
THEIR FATHER	NAME	NAME	NAME
NAME	BORN	BORN	LIVED
BORN	DIED	DIED	NAME
DIED	MARRIED	MARRIED	LIVED
MARRIED	NOTES	NAME	NAME
NOTES		BORN	LIVED
		DIED	NAME
		NOTES	LIVED
	NAME	NAME	NAME
	BORN	BORN	LIVED
	DIED	DIED	NAME
	NOTES	MARRIED	LIVED
		NAME	NAME
		BORN	LIVED
		DIED	NAME
		NOTES	LIVED
THEIR MOTHER	NAME	NAME	NAME
NAME	BORN	BORN	LIVED
BORN	DIED	DIED	NAME
DIED	MARRIED	MARRIED	LIVED
NOTES	NOTES	NAME	NAME
		BORN	LIVED
		DIED	NAME
		NOTES	LIVED
	NAME	NAME	NAME
	BORN	BORN	LIVED
	DIED	DIED	NAME
	NOTES	MARRIED	LIVED
		NAME	NAME
		BORN	LIVED
		DIED	NAME
		NOTES	LIVED

| 6X GREAT-GRANDPARENTS | 7X GREAT-GRANDPARENTS | 8X GREAT-GRANDPARENTS | 9X GREAT-GRANDPARENTS |

THIS CHART STARTS WITH THE PARENTS OF 231.

9th GENERATION	10th GENERATION	11th GENERATION	12th GENERATION
THEIR FATHER	NAME	NAME	NAME
NAME	BORN	BORN	LIVED
BORN	DIED	DIED	NAME
DIED	MARRIED	MARRIED	LIVED
MARRIED	NOTES	NAME	NAME
NOTES		BORN	LIVED
		DIED	NAME
		NOTES	LIVED
	NAME	NAME	NAME
	BORN	BORN	LIVED
	DIED	DIED	NAME
	NOTES	MARRIED	LIVED
		NAME	NAME
		BORN	LIVED
		DIED	NAME
		NOTES	LIVED
THEIR MOTHER	NAME	NAME	NAME
NAME	BORN	BORN	LIVED
BORN	DIED	DIED	NAME
DIED	MARRIED	MARRIED	LIVED
NOTES	NOTES	NAME	NAME
		BORN	LIVED
		DIED	NAME
		NOTES	LIVED
	NAME	NAME	NAME
	BORN	BORN	LIVED
	DIED	DIED	NAME
	NOTES	MARRIED	LIVED
		NAME	NAME
		BORN	LIVED
		DIED	NAME
		NOTES	LIVED

6X GREAT-GRANDPARENTS	7X GREAT-GRANDPARENTS	8X GREAT-GRANDPARENTS	9X GREAT-GRANDPARENTS

9th GENERATION	10th GENERATION	11th GENERATION	12th GENERATION
THEIR FATHER	NAME	NAME	NAME
NAME	BORN	BORN	LIVED
BORN	DIED	DIED	NAME
DIED	MARRIED	MARRIED	LIVED
MARRIED	NOTES	NAME	NAME
NOTES		BORN	LIVED
		DIED	NAME
		NOTES	LIVED
	NAME	NAME	NAME
	BORN	BORN	LIVED
	DIED	DIED	NAME
	NOTES	MARRIED	LIVED
		NAME	NAME
		BORN	LIVED
		DIED	NAME
		NOTES	LIVED
THEIR MOTHER	NAME	NAME	NAME
NAME	BORN	BORN	LIVED
BORN	DIED	DIED	NAME
DIED	MARRIED	MARRIED	LIVED
NOTES	NOTES	NAME	NAME
		BORN	LIVED
		DIED	NAME
		NOTES	LIVED
	NAME	NAME	NAME
	BORN	BORN	LIVED
	DIED	DIED	NAME
	NOTES	MARRIED	LIVED
		NAME	NAME
		BORN	LIVED
		DIED	NAME
		NOTES	LIVED

6X GREAT-GRANDPARENTS	7X GREAT-GRANDPARENTS	8X GREAT-GRANDPARENTS	9X GREAT-GRANDPARENTS

THIS CHART STARTS WITH THE PARENTS OF 233.

9th GENERATION	10th GENERATION	11th GENERATION	12th GENERATION
THEIR FATHER	NAME	NAME	NAME
NAME	BORN	BORN	LIVED
BORN	DIED	DIED	NAME
DIED	MARRIED	MARRIED	LIVED
MARRIED	NOTES	NAME	NAME
NOTES		BORN	LIVED
		DIED	NAME
		NOTES	LIVED
	NAME	NAME	NAME
	BORN	BORN	LIVED
	DIED	DIED	NAME
	NOTES	MARRIED	LIVED
		NAME	NAME
		BORN	LIVED
		DIED	NAME
		NOTES	LIVED
THEIR MOTHER	NAME	NAME	NAME
NAME	BORN	BORN	LIVED
BORN	DIED	DIED	NAME
DIED	MARRIED	MARRIED	LIVED
NOTES	NOTES	NAME	NAME
		BORN	LIVED
		DIED	NAME
		NOTES	LIVED
	NAME	NAME	NAME
	BORN	BORN	LIVED
	DIED	DIED	NAME
	NOTES	MARRIED	LIVED
		NAME	NAME
		BORN	LIVED
		DIED	NAME
		NOTES	LIVED

| 6X GREAT-GRANDPARENTS | 7X GREAT-GRANDPARENTS | 8X GREAT-GRANDPARENTS | 9X GREAT-GRANDPARENTS |

9th GENERATION	10th GENERATION	11th GENERATION	12th GENERATION
THEIR FATHER	NAME	NAME	NAME
NAME	BORN	BORN	LIVED
BORN	DIED	DIED	NAME
DIED	MARRIED	MARRIED	LIVED
MARRIED	NOTES	NAME	NAME
NOTES		BORN	LIVED
		DIED	NAME
		NOTES	LIVED
	NAME	NAME	NAME
	BORN	BORN	LIVED
	DIED	DIED	NAME
	NOTES	MARRIED	LIVED
		NAME	NAME
		BORN	LIVED
		DIED	NAME
		NOTES	LIVED
THEIR MOTHER	NAME	NAME	NAME
NAME	BORN	BORN	LIVED
BORN	DIED	DIED	NAME
DIED	MARRIED	MARRIED	LIVED
NOTES	NOTES	NAME	NAME
		BORN	LIVED
		DIED	NAME
		NOTES	LIVED
	NAME	NAME	NAME
	BORN	BORN	LIVED
	DIED	DIED	NAME
	NOTES	MARRIED	LIVED
		NAME	NAME
		BORN	LIVED
		DIED	NAME
		NOTES	LIVED

| 6X GREAT-GRANDPARENTS | 7X GREAT-GRANDPARENTS | 8X GREAT-GRANDPARENTS | 9X GREAT-GRANDPARENTS |

THIS CHART STARTS WITH THE PARENTS OF 235.

9th GENERATION	10th GENERATION	11th GENERATION	12th GENERATION
THEIR FATHER NAME BORN DIED MARRIED NOTES	NAME BORN DIED MARRIED NOTES	NAME BORN DIED MARRIED	NAME LIVED
			NAME LIVED
		NAME BORN DIED NOTES	NAME LIVED
			NAME LIVED
	NAME BORN DIED NOTES	NAME BORN DIED MARRIED	NAME LIVED
			NAME LIVED
		NAME BORN DIED NOTES	NAME LIVED
			NAME LIVED
THEIR MOTHER NAME BORN DIED NOTES	NAME BORN DIED MARRIED NOTES	NAME BORN DIED MARRIED	NAME LIVED
			NAME LIVED
		NAME BORN DIED NOTES	NAME LIVED
			NAME LIVED
	NAME BORN DIED NOTES	NAME BORN DIED MARRIED	NAME LIVED
			NAME LIVED
		NAME BORN DIED NOTES	NAME LIVED
			NAME LIVED
6X GREAT-GRANDPARENTS	7X GREAT-GRANDPARENTS	8X GREAT-GRANDPARENTS	9X GREAT-GRANDPARENTS

9th GENERATION	10th GENERATION	11th GENERATION	12th GENERATION
THEIR FATHER	NAME	NAME	NAME
NAME	BORN	BORN	LIVED
BORN	DIED	DIED	NAME
DIED	MARRIED	MARRIED	LIVED
MARRIED	NOTES	NAME	NAME
NOTES		BORN	LIVED
		DIED	NAME
		NOTES	LIVED
	NAME	NAME	NAME
	BORN	BORN	LIVED
	DIED	DIED	NAME
	NOTES	MARRIED	LIVED
		NAME	NAME
		BORN	LIVED
		DIED	NAME
		NOTES	LIVED
THEIR MOTHER	NAME	NAME	NAME
NAME	BORN	BORN	LIVED
BORN	DIED	DIED	NAME
DIED	MARRIED	MARRIED	LIVED
NOTES	NOTES	NAME	NAME
		BORN	LIVED
		DIED	NAME
		NOTES	LIVED
	NAME	NAME	NAME
	BORN	BORN	LIVED
	DIED	DIED	NAME
	NOTES	MARRIED	LIVED
		NAME	NAME
		BORN	LIVED
		DIED	NAME
		NOTES	LIVED

| 6X GREAT-GRANDPARENTS | 7X GREAT-GRANDPARENTS | 8X GREAT-GRANDPARENTS | 9X GREAT-GRANDPARENTS |

9th GENERATION	10th GENERATION	11th GENERATION	12th GENERATION
THEIR FATHER	NAME	NAME	NAME
NAME	BORN	BORN	LIVED
BORN	DIED	DIED	NAME
DIED	MARRIED	MARRIED	LIVED
MARRIED	NOTES	NAME	NAME
NOTES		BORN	LIVED
		DIED	NAME
		NOTES	LIVED
	NAME	NAME	NAME
	BORN	BORN	LIVED
	DIED	DIED	NAME
	NOTES	MARRIED	LIVED
		NAME	NAME
		BORN	LIVED
		DIED	NAME
		NOTES	LIVED
THEIR MOTHER	NAME	NAME	NAME
NAME	BORN	BORN	LIVED
BORN	DIED	DIED	NAME
DIED	MARRIED	MARRIED	LIVED
NOTES	NOTES	NAME	NAME
		BORN	LIVED
		DIED	NAME
		NOTES	LIVED
	NAME	NAME	NAME
	BORN	BORN	LIVED
	DIED	DIED	NAME
	NOTES	MARRIED	LIVED
		NAME	NAME
		BORN	LIVED
		DIED	NAME
		NOTES	LIVED

| 6X GREAT-GRANDPARENTS | 7X GREAT-GRANDPARENTS | 8X GREAT-GRANDPARENTS | 9X GREAT-GRANDPARENTS |

THIS CHART STARTS WITH THE PARENTS OF 238.

9th GENERATION	10th GENERATION	11th GENERATION	12th GENERATION
THEIR FATHER	NAME	NAME	NAME
NAME	BORN	BORN	LIVED
BORN	DIED	DIED	NAME
DIED	MARRIED	MARRIED	LIVED
MARRIED	NOTES	NAME	NAME
NOTES		BORN	LIVED
		DIED	NAME
		NOTES	LIVED
	NAME	NAME	NAME
	BORN	BORN	LIVED
	DIED	DIED	NAME
	NOTES	MARRIED	LIVED
		NAME	NAME
		BORN	LIVED
		DIED	NAME
		NOTES	LIVED
THEIR MOTHER	NAME	NAME	NAME
NAME	BORN	BORN	LIVED
BORN	DIED	DIED	NAME
DIED	MARRIED	MARRIED	LIVED
NOTES	NOTES	NAME	NAME
		BORN	LIVED
		DIED	NAME
		NOTES	LIVED
	NAME	NAME	NAME
	BORN	BORN	LIVED
	DIED	DIED	NAME
	NOTES	MARRIED	LIVED
		NAME	NAME
		BORN	LIVED
		DIED	NAME
		NOTES	LIVED

| 6X GREAT-GRANDPARENTS | 7X GREAT-GRANDPARENTS | 8X GREAT-GRANDPARENTS | 9X GREAT-GRANDPARENTS |

THIS CHART STARTS WITH THE PARENTS OF 239.

9th GENERATION	10th GENERATION	11th GENERATION	12th GENERATION
THEIR FATHER	NAME	NAME	NAME
NAME	BORN	BORN	LIVED
BORN	DIED	DIED	NAME
DIED	MARRIED	MARRIED	LIVED
MARRIED	NOTES	NAME	NAME
NOTES		BORN	LIVED
		DIED	NAME
		NOTES	LIVED
	NAME	NAME	NAME
	BORN	BORN	LIVED
	DIED	DIED	NAME
	NOTES	MARRIED	LIVED
		NAME	NAME
		BORN	LIVED
		DIED	NAME
		NOTES	LIVED
THEIR MOTHER	NAME	NAME	NAME
NAME	BORN	BORN	LIVED
BORN	DIED	DIED	NAME
DIED	MARRIED	MARRIED	LIVED
NOTES	NOTES	NAME	NAME
		BORN	LIVED
		DIED	NAME
		NOTES	LIVED
	NAME	NAME	NAME
	BORN	BORN	LIVED
	DIED	DIED	NAME
	NOTES	MARRIED	LIVED
		NAME	NAME
		BORN	LIVED
		DIED	NAME
		NOTES	LIVED

6X GREAT-GRANDPARENTS	7X GREAT-GRANDPARENTS	8X GREAT-GRANDPARENTS	9X GREAT-GRANDPARENTS

THIS CHART STARTS WITH THE PARENTS OF 240.

9th GENERATION	10th GENERATION	11th GENERATION	12th GENERATION
THEIR FATHER	NAME	NAME	NAME
NAME	BORN	BORN	LIVED
BORN	DIED	DIED	NAME
DIED	MARRIED	MARRIED	LIVED
MARRIED	NOTES	NAME	NAME
NOTES		BORN	LIVED
		DIED	NAME
		NOTES	LIVED
	NAME	NAME	NAME
	BORN	BORN	LIVED
	DIED	DIED	NAME
	NOTES	MARRIED	LIVED
		NAME	NAME
		BORN	LIVED
		DIED	NAME
		NOTES	LIVED
THEIR MOTHER	NAME	NAME	NAME
NAME	BORN	BORN	LIVED
BORN	DIED	DIED	NAME
DIED	MARRIED	MARRIED	LIVED
NOTES	NOTES	NAME	NAME
		BORN	LIVED
		DIED	NAME
		NOTES	LIVED
	NAME	NAME	NAME
	BORN	BORN	LIVED
	DIED	DIED	NAME
	NOTES	MARRIED	LIVED
		NAME	NAME
		BORN	LIVED
		DIED	NAME
		NOTES	LIVED

| 6X GREAT-GRANDPARENTS | 7X GREAT-GRANDPARENTS | 8X GREAT-GRANDPARENTS | 9X GREAT-GRANDPARENTS |

THIS CHART STARTS WITH THE PARENTS OF 241.

9th GENERATION	10th GENERATION	11th GENERATION	12th GENERATION
THEIR FATHER NAME BORN DIED MARRIED NOTES	NAME BORN DIED MARRIED NOTES	NAME BORN DIED MARRIED	NAME LIVED
			NAME LIVED
		NAME BORN DIED NOTES	NAME LIVED
			NAME LIVED
	NAME BORN DIED NOTES	NAME BORN DIED MARRIED	NAME LIVED
			NAME LIVED
		NAME BORN DIED NOTES	NAME LIVED
			NAME LIVED
THEIR MOTHER NAME BORN DIED NOTES	NAME BORN DIED MARRIED NOTES	NAME BORN DIED MARRIED	NAME LIVED
			NAME LIVED
		NAME BORN DIED NOTES	NAME LIVED
			NAME LIVED
	NAME BORN DIED NOTES	NAME BORN DIED MARRIED	NAME LIVED
			NAME LIVED
		NAME BORN DIED NOTES	NAME LIVED
			NAME LIVED
6X GREAT-GRANDPARENTS	7X GREAT-GRANDPARENTS	8X GREAT-GRANDPARENTS	9X GREAT-GRANDPARENTS

9th GENERATION	10th GENERATION	11th GENERATION	12th GENERATION
THEIR FATHER	NAME	NAME	NAME
NAME	BORN	BORN	LIVED
BORN	DIED	DIED	NAME
DIED	MARRIED	MARRIED	LIVED
MARRIED	NOTES	NAME	NAME
NOTES		BORN	LIVED
		DIED	NAME
		NOTES	LIVED
	NAME	NAME	NAME
	BORN	BORN	LIVED
	DIED	DIED	NAME
	NOTES	MARRIED	LIVED
		NAME	NAME
		BORN	LIVED
		DIED	NAME
		NOTES	LIVED
THEIR MOTHER	NAME	NAME	NAME
NAME	BORN	BORN	LIVED
BORN	DIED	DIED	NAME
DIED	MARRIED	MARRIED	LIVED
NOTES	NOTES	NAME	NAME
		BORN	LIVED
		DIED	NAME
		NOTES	LIVED
	NAME	NAME	NAME
	BORN	BORN	LIVED
	DIED	DIED	NAME
	NOTES	MARRIED	LIVED
		NAME	NAME
		BORN	LIVED
		DIED	NAME
		NOTES	LIVED

6X GREAT-GRANDPARENTS	7X GREAT-GRANDPARENTS	8X GREAT-GRANDPARENTS	9X GREAT-GRANDPARENTS

THIS CHART STARTS WITH THE PARENTS OF 243.

9th GENERATION	10th GENERATION	11th GENERATION	12th GENERATION
THEIR FATHER	NAME	NAME	NAME
NAME	BORN	BORN	LIVED
BORN	DIED	DIED	NAME
DIED	MARRIED	MARRIED	LIVED
MARRIED	NOTES	NAME	NAME
NOTES		BORN	LIVED
		DIED	NAME
		NOTES	LIVED
	NAME	NAME	NAME
	BORN	BORN	LIVED
	DIED	DIED	NAME
	NOTES	MARRIED	LIVED
		NAME	NAME
		BORN	LIVED
		DIED	NAME
		NOTES	LIVED
THEIR MOTHER	NAME	NAME	NAME
NAME	BORN	BORN	LIVED
BORN	DIED	DIED	NAME
DIED	MARRIED	MARRIED	LIVED
NOTES	NOTES	NAME	NAME
		BORN	LIVED
		DIED	NAME
		NOTES	LIVED
	NAME	NAME	NAME
	BORN	BORN	LIVED
	DIED	DIED	NAME
	NOTES	MARRIED	LIVED
		NAME	NAME
		BORN	LIVED
		DIED	NAME
		NOTES	LIVED

| 6X GREAT-GRANDPARENTS | 7X GREAT-GRANDPARENTS | 8X GREAT-GRANDPARENTS | 9X GREAT-GRANDPARENTS |

THIS CHART STARTS WITH THE PARENTS OF 244.

9th GENERATION	10th GENERATION	11th GENERATION	12th GENERATION
THEIR FATHER NAME BORN DIED MARRIED NOTES	NAME BORN DIED MARRIED NOTES	NAME BORN DIED MARRIED	NAME LIVED
			NAME LIVED
		NAME BORN DIED NOTES	NAME LIVED
			NAME LIVED
	NAME BORN DIED NOTES	NAME BORN DIED MARRIED	NAME LIVED
			NAME LIVED
		NAME BORN DIED NOTES	NAME LIVED
			NAME LIVED
THEIR MOTHER NAME BORN DIED NOTES	NAME BORN DIED MARRIED NOTES	NAME BORN DIED MARRIED	NAME LIVED
			NAME LIVED
		NAME BORN DIED NOTES	NAME LIVED
			NAME LIVED
	NAME BORN DIED NOTES	NAME BORN DIED MARRIED	NAME LIVED
			NAME LIVED
		NAME BORN DIED NOTES	NAME LIVED
			NAME LIVED
6X GREAT-GRANDPARENTS	7X GREAT-GRANDPARENTS	8X GREAT-GRANDPARENTS	9X GREAT-GRANDPARENTS

THIS CHART STARTS WITH THE PARENTS OF 245.

9th GENERATION	10th GENERATION	11th GENERATION	12th GENERATION
THEIR FATHER	NAME	NAME	NAME
NAME	BORN	BORN	LIVED
BORN	DIED	DIED	NAME
DIED	MARRIED	MARRIED	LIVED
MARRIED	NOTES	NAME	NAME
NOTES		BORN	LIVED
		DIED	NAME
		NOTES	LIVED
	NAME	NAME	NAME
	BORN	BORN	LIVED
	DIED	DIED	NAME
	NOTES	MARRIED	LIVED
		NAME	NAME
		BORN	LIVED
		DIED	NAME
		NOTES	LIVED
THEIR MOTHER	NAME	NAME	NAME
NAME	BORN	BORN	LIVED
BORN	DIED	DIED	NAME
DIED	MARRIED	MARRIED	LIVED
NOTES	NOTES	NAME	NAME
		BORN	LIVED
		DIED	NAME
		NOTES	LIVED
	NAME	NAME	NAME
	BORN	BORN	LIVED
	DIED	DIED	NAME
	NOTES	MARRIED	LIVED
		NAME	NAME
		BORN	LIVED
		DIED	NAME
		NOTES	LIVED

| 6X GREAT-GRANDPARENTS | 7X GREAT-GRANDPARENTS | 8X GREAT-GRANDPARENTS | 9X GREAT-GRANDPARENTS |

THIS CHART STARTS WITH THE PARENTS OF 246.

9th GENERATION	10th GENERATION	11th GENERATION	12th GENERATION
THEIR FATHER	NAME	NAME	NAME
NAME	BORN	BORN	LIVED
BORN	DIED	DIED	NAME
DIED	MARRIED	MARRIED	LIVED
MARRIED	NOTES	NAME	NAME
NOTES		BORN	LIVED
		DIED	NAME
		NOTES	LIVED
	NAME	NAME	NAME
	BORN	BORN	LIVED
	DIED	DIED	NAME
	NOTES	MARRIED	LIVED
		NAME	NAME
		BORN	LIVED
		DIED	NAME
		NOTES	LIVED
THEIR MOTHER	NAME	NAME	NAME
NAME	BORN	BORN	LIVED
BORN	DIED	DIED	NAME
DIED	MARRIED	MARRIED	LIVED
NOTES	NOTES	NAME	NAME
		BORN	LIVED
		DIED	NAME
		NOTES	LIVED
	NAME	NAME	NAME
	BORN	BORN	LIVED
	DIED	DIED	NAME
	NOTES	MARRIED	LIVED
		NAME	NAME
		BORN	LIVED
		DIED	NAME
		NOTES	LIVED

6X GREAT-GRANDPARENTS	7X GREAT-GRANDPARENTS	8X GREAT-GRANDPARENTS	9X GREAT-GRANDPARENTS

THIS CHART STARTS WITH THE PARENTS OF 247

9th GENERATION	10th GENERATION	11th GENERATION	12th GENERATION
THEIR FATHER	NAME	NAME	NAME
NAME	BORN	BORN	LIVED
BORN	DIED	DIED	NAME
DIED	MARRIED	MARRIED	LIVED
MARRIED	NOTES	NAME	NAME
NOTES		BORN	LIVED
		DIED	NAME
		NOTES	LIVED
	NAME	NAME	NAME
	BORN	BORN	LIVED
	DIED	DIED	NAME
	NOTES	MARRIED	LIVED
		NAME	NAME
		BORN	LIVED
		DIED	NAME
		NOTES	LIVED
THEIR MOTHER	NAME	NAME	NAME
NAME	BORN	BORN	LIVED
BORN	DIED	DIED	NAME
DIED	MARRIED	MARRIED	LIVED
NOTES	NOTES	NAME	NAME
		BORN	LIVED
		DIED	NAME
		NOTES	LIVED
	NAME	NAME	NAME
	BORN	BORN	LIVED
	DIED	DIED	NAME
	NOTES	MARRIED	LIVED
		NAME	NAME
		BORN	LIVED
		DIED	NAME
		NOTES	LIVED

6X GREAT-GRANDPARENTS	7X GREAT-GRANDPARENTS	8X GREAT-GRANDPARENTS	9X GREAT-GRANDPARENTS

9th GENERATION	10th GENERATION	11th GENERATION	12th GENERATION
THEIR FATHER	NAME	NAME	NAME
NAME	BORN	BORN	LIVED
BORN	DIED	DIED	NAME
DIED	MARRIED	MARRIED	LIVED
MARRIED	NOTES	NAME	NAME
NOTES		BORN	LIVED
		DIED	NAME
		NOTES	LIVED
	NAME	NAME	NAME
	BORN	BORN	LIVED
	DIED	DIED	NAME
	NOTES	MARRIED	LIVED
		NAME	NAME
		BORN	LIVED
		DIED	NAME
		NOTES	LIVED
THEIR MOTHER	NAME	NAME	NAME
NAME	BORN	BORN	LIVED
BORN	DIED	DIED	NAME
DIED	MARRIED	MARRIED	LIVED
NOTES	NOTES	NAME	NAME
		BORN	LIVED
		DIED	NAME
		NOTES	LIVED
	NAME	NAME	NAME
	BORN	BORN	LIVED
	DIED	DIED	NAME
	NOTES	MARRIED	LIVED
		NAME	NAME
		BORN	LIVED
		DIED	NAME
		NOTES	LIVED

6X GREAT-GRANDPARENTS	7X GREAT-GRANDPARENTS	8X GREAT-GRANDPARENTS	9X GREAT-GRANDPARENTS

THIS CHART STARTS WITH THE PARENTS OF 249.

9th GENERATION	10th GENERATION	11th GENERATION	12th GENERATION
THEIR FATHER NAME BORN DIED MARRIED NOTES	NAME BORN DIED MARRIED NOTES	NAME BORN DIED MARRIED	NAME LIVED NAME LIVED
		NAME BORN DIED NOTES	NAME LIVED NAME LIVED
	NAME BORN DIED NOTES	NAME BORN DIED MARRIED	NAME LIVED NAME LIVED
		NAME BORN DIED NOTES	NAME LIVED NAME LIVED
THEIR MOTHER NAME BORN DIED NOTES	NAME BORN DIED MARRIED NOTES	NAME BORN DIED MARRIED	NAME LIVED NAME LIVED
		NAME BORN DIED NOTES	NAME LIVED NAME LIVED
	NAME BORN DIED NOTES	NAME BORN DIED MARRIED	NAME LIVED NAME LIVED
		NAME BORN DIED NOTES	NAME LIVED NAME LIVED

| 6X GREAT-GRANDPARENTS | 7X GREAT-GRANDPARENTS | 8X GREAT-GRANDPARENTS | 9X GREAT-GRANDPARENTS |

THIS CHART STARTS WITH THE PARENTS OF 250.

9th GENERATION	10th GENERATION	11th GENERATION	12th GENERATION
THEIR FATHER	NAME	NAME	NAME
NAME	BORN	BORN	LIVED
BORN	DIED	DIED	NAME
DIED	MARRIED	MARRIED	LIVED
MARRIED	NOTES	NAME	NAME
NOTES		BORN	LIVED
		DIED	NAME
		NOTES	LIVED
	NAME	NAME	NAME
	BORN	BORN	LIVED
	DIED	DIED	NAME
	NOTES	MARRIED	LIVED
		NAME	NAME
		BORN	LIVED
		DIED	NAME
		NOTES	LIVED
THEIR MOTHER	NAME	NAME	NAME
NAME	BORN	BORN	LIVED
BORN	DIED	DIED	NAME
DIED	MARRIED	MARRIED	LIVED
NOTES	NOTES	NAME	NAME
		BORN	LIVED
		DIED	NAME
		NOTES	LIVED
	NAME	NAME	NAME
	BORN	BORN	LIVED
	DIED	DIED	NAME
	NOTES	MARRIED	LIVED
		NAME	NAME
		BORN	LIVED
		DIED	NAME
		NOTES	LIVED

| 6X GREAT-GRANDPARENTS | 7X GREAT-GRANDPARENTS | 8X GREAT-GRANDPARENTS | 9X GREAT-GRANDPARENTS |

THIS CHART STARTS WITH THE PARENTS OF 251.

9th GENERATION	10th GENERATION	11th GENERATION	12th GENERATION
THEIR FATHER	NAME	NAME	NAME
NAME	BORN	BORN	LIVED
BORN	DIED	DIED	NAME
DIED	MARRIED	MARRIED	LIVED
MARRIED	NOTES	NAME	NAME
NOTES		BORN	LIVED
		DIED	NAME
		NOTES	LIVED
	NAME	NAME	NAME
	BORN	BORN	LIVED
	DIED	DIED	NAME
	NOTES	MARRIED	LIVED
		NAME	NAME
		BORN	LIVED
		DIED	NAME
		NOTES	LIVED
THEIR MOTHER	NAME	NAME	NAME
NAME	BORN	BORN	LIVED
BORN	DIED	DIED	NAME
DIED	MARRIED	MARRIED	LIVED
NOTES	NOTES	NAME	NAME
		BORN	LIVED
		DIED	NAME
		NOTES	LIVED
	NAME	NAME	NAME
	BORN	BORN	LIVED
	DIED	DIED	NAME
	NOTES	MARRIED	LIVED
		NAME	NAME
		BORN	LIVED
		DIED	NAME
		NOTES	LIVED

6X GREAT-GRANDPARENTS	7X GREAT-GRANDPARENTS	8X GREAT-GRANDPARENTS	9X GREAT-GRANDPARENTS

THIS CHART STARTS WITH THE PARENTS OF 252.

9th GENERATION	10th GENERATION	11th GENERATION	12th GENERATION
THEIR FATHER NAME BORN DIED MARRIED NOTES	NAME BORN DIED MARRIED NOTES	NAME BORN DIED MARRIED	NAME LIVED
			NAME LIVED
		NAME BORN DIED NOTES	NAME LIVED
			NAME LIVED
	NAME BORN DIED NOTES	NAME BORN DIED MARRIED	NAME LIVED
			NAME LIVED
		NAME BORN DIED NOTES	NAME LIVED
			NAME LIVED
THEIR MOTHER NAME BORN DIED NOTES	NAME BORN DIED MARRIED NOTES	NAME BORN DIED MARRIED	NAME LIVED
			NAME LIVED
		NAME BORN DIED NOTES	NAME LIVED
			NAME LIVED
	NAME BORN DIED NOTES	NAME BORN DIED MARRIED	NAME LIVED
			NAME LIVED
		NAME BORN DIED NOTES	NAME LIVED
			NAME LIVED

| 6X GREAT-GRANDPARENTS | 7X GREAT-GRANDPARENTS | 8X GREAT-GRANDPARENTS | 9X GREAT-GRANDPARENTS |

THIS CHART STARTS WITH THE PARENTS OF 253.

9th GENERATION	10th GENERATION	11th GENERATION	12th GENERATION
THEIR FATHER	NAME	NAME	NAME
NAME	BORN	BORN	LIVED
BORN	DIED	DIED	NAME
DIED	MARRIED	MARRIED	LIVED
MARRIED	NOTES	NAME	NAME
NOTES		BORN	LIVED
		DIED	NAME
		NOTES	LIVED
	NAME	NAME	NAME
	BORN	BORN	LIVED
	DIED	DIED	NAME
	NOTES	MARRIED	LIVED
		NAME	NAME
		BORN	LIVED
		DIED	NAME
		NOTES	LIVED
THEIR MOTHER	NAME	NAME	NAME
NAME	BORN	BORN	LIVED
BORN	DIED	DIED	NAME
DIED	MARRIED	MARRIED	LIVED
NOTES	NOTES	NAME	NAME
		BORN	LIVED
		DIED	NAME
		NOTES	LIVED
	NAME	NAME	NAME
	BORN	BORN	LIVED
	DIED	DIED	NAME
	NOTES	MARRIED	LIVED
		NAME	NAME
		BORN	LIVED
		DIED	NAME
		NOTES	LIVED

6X GREAT-GRANDPARENTS	7X GREAT-GRANDPARENTS	8X GREAT-GRANDPARENTS	9X GREAT-GRANDPARENTS

9th GENERATION	10th GENERATION	11th GENERATION	12th GENERATION
THEIR FATHER	NAME	NAME	NAME
NAME	BORN	BORN	LIVED
BORN	DIED	DIED	NAME
DIED	MARRIED	MARRIED	LIVED
MARRIED	NOTES	NAME	NAME
NOTES		BORN	LIVED
		DIED	NAME
		NOTES	LIVED
	NAME	NAME	NAME
	BORN	BORN	LIVED
	DIED	DIED	NAME
	NOTES	MARRIED	LIVED
		NAME	NAME
		BORN	LIVED
		DIED	NAME
		NOTES	LIVED
THEIR MOTHER	NAME	NAME	NAME
NAME	BORN	BORN	LIVED
BORN	DIED	DIED	NAME
DIED	MARRIED	MARRIED	LIVED
NOTES	NOTES	NAME	NAME
		BORN	LIVED
		DIED	NAME
		NOTES	LIVED
	NAME	NAME	NAME
	BORN	BORN	LIVED
	DIED	DIED	NAME
	NOTES	MARRIED	LIVED
		NAME	NAME
		BORN	LIVED
		DIED	NAME
		NOTES	LIVED

| 6X GREAT-GRANDPARENTS | 7X GREAT-GRANDPARENTS | 8X GREAT-GRANDPARENTS | 9X GREAT-GRANDPARENTS |

9th GENERATION	10th GENERATION	11th GENERATION	12th GENERATION
THEIR FATHER	NAME	NAME	NAME
NAME	BORN	BORN	LIVED
BORN	DIED	DIED	NAME
DIED	MARRIED	MARRIED	LIVED
MARRIED	NOTES	NAME	NAME
NOTES		BORN	LIVED
		DIED	NAME
		NOTES	LIVED
	NAME	NAME	NAME
	BORN	BORN	LIVED
	DIED	DIED	NAME
	NOTES	MARRIED	LIVED
		NAME	NAME
		BORN	LIVED
		DIED	NAME
		NOTES	LIVED
THEIR MOTHER	NAME	NAME	NAME
NAME	BORN	BORN	LIVED
BORN	DIED	DIED	NAME
DIED	MARRIED	MARRIED	LIVED
NOTES	NOTES	NAME	NAME
		BORN	LIVED
		DIED	NAME
		NOTES	LIVED
	NAME	NAME	NAME
	BORN	BORN	LIVED
	DIED	DIED	NAME
	NOTES	MARRIED	LIVED
		NAME	NAME
		BORN	LIVED
		DIED	NAME
		NOTES	LIVED

6X GREAT-GRANDPARENTS	7X GREAT-GRANDPARENTS	8X GREAT-GRANDPARENTS	9X GREAT-GRANDPARENTS

NOTES

NOTES

NOTES

NOTES

NOTES

OUR
FAMILY TREE

This   family history
was compiled by
in the year(s)
Valuable contributions were made by:

This book was designed by the artist Sarah Zar for House Elves Anonymous, a project devoted to creating museum-quality family heirlooms and useful genealogy research materials. S. Zar's website is SarahZar.com.

You can order the family tree poster that matches this book, and purchase additional copies of "Our Family Tree Index" at **HouseElvesAnonymous.com**. Both are available in digital and print format.

COUSIN CHART

OF FAMILY RELATIONSHIPS

ONCE REMOVED = One generation away from you.
% = Shared DNA between you and your blood relative.

					GREAT GREAT GREAT GRANDPARENT 3.125%
				GREAT GREAT GRANDPARENT 6.5%	THIRD GREAT AUNT or UNCLE 3.125%
			GREAT GRANDPARENT 12.5%	GREAT GREAT AUNT or UNCLE 6.5%	1st COUSIN 3x removed 1.563%
		GRANDPARENT 25%	GREAT AUNT or UNCLE 12.5%	1st COUSIN twice removed 3.125%	2nd COUSIN twice removed 0.781%
	PARENT 50%	AUNT or UNCLE 25%	1st COUSIN once removed 6.5%	2nd COUSIN once removed 1.563%	3rd COUSIN once removed 0.391%
YOU ARE HERE	SIBLING 50%	1st COUSIN 12.5%	2nd COUSIN 3.125%	3rd COUSIN 0.781%	4th COUSIN 0.195%
CHILD 50%	NIECE or NEPHEW 25%	1st COUSIN once removed 6.25%	2nd COUSIN once removed 1.563%	3rd COUSIN once removed 0.391%	4th COUSIN once removed 0.0977%
GRANDCHILD 25%	GREAT NIECE or NEPHEW 12.5%	1st COUSIN twice removed 3.125%	2nd COUSIN twice removed 0.781%	3rd COUSIN twice removed 0.195%	4th COUSIN twice removed 0.0488%

IN THESE 12

GENERATIONS...

OF

GEN.	FAMILY RELATIONSHIP	# IN THIS GENERATION	CUMULATIVE	~ BIRTH YEAR
1	First person in tree	1	1	x
2	Parents	2	3	x - 30
3	Grandparents	4	7	x - 60
4	Great-grandparents	8	15	x - 90
5	2 times great-grandparents	16	31	x - 120
6	3 times great-grandparents	32	63	x - 150
7	4 times great-grandparents	64	127	x - 180
8	5 times great-grandparents	128	255	x - 210
9	6 times great-grandparents	256	511	x - 240
10	7 times great-grandparents	512	1023	x - 270
11	8 times great-grandparents	1024	2047	x - 300
12	9 times great-grandparents	2048	4095	x - 330

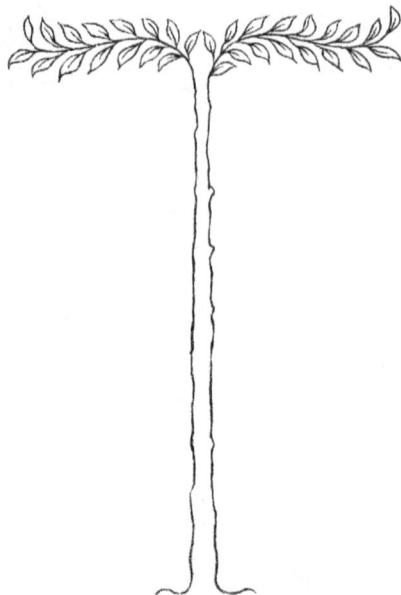

TO BE
CONTINUED...